Bible Fun Stuff

FOR MIDDLE SCHOOL

Action!
Cool Theater

ACTION! COOL THEATER
Published by David C. Cook
4050 Lee Vance View
Colorado Springs, CO 80918 U.S.A.

David C. Cook Distribution Canada
55 Woodslee Avenue, Paris, Ontario, Canada N3L 3E5

David C. Cook U.K., Kingsway Communications
Eastbourne, East Sussex BN23 6NT, England

David C. Cook and the graphic circle C logo
Are registered trademarks of Cook Communications Ministries.

Written by Caroline Ferdinandsen
Cover Design by BMB Design
Cover Photography © Brad Armstrong Photography
Interior Design by Rebekah Lyon
Illustrations by Hector Adrian Borlasca

ISBN 978-1-4347-6856-8

Printed in United States
First Printing 2008

1 2 3 4 5 6 7 8 9 10

FOR MIDDLE SCHOOL

Action! Cool Theater

Table of Contents

Introduction 5

Patrick the Powerful and the Kid Kingdom *1 Samuel 8:4-10, 19-22*
Students lead a revolt against their teacher, putting one of their own in charge.........................6

Light Fraud Speaks Out *1 Samuel 28:1a, 3-19*
Light Fraud speaks so-called "truth," but it is really darkness in disguise.........................10

Wisdom Walks the Red Carpet *1 Kings 3:5-14*
Like the Oscars? Students participate in a Proverbs "Film Festival" 14

The Advice Is Right *1 Kings 12:3-16*
Teens act out a game show, "The Advice Is Right," and learn to win with good judgment.........................18

Worship Isn't for Spectators *2 Chronicles 5:12-13; Ezra 3:10-11; 1 Corinthians 14:15, 26-33*
Kids plan a Creative Worship Festival using songs, dance, poetry, artwork, and more! 22

Jumping Jehoshaphat *2 Chronicles 17:1-10*
Meet King J-Dogg—a monologue of King Jehoshaphat, with a modern twist! 26

Courtly Courage *Esther 2:5-10; 3:1, 5-6, 13; 4:13-16*
With promptings, students perform an improvised version of the Esther story 30

America's Next Best Friend *Psalms 34:17-18; 55:16-17; 1 Thessalonians 5:17;*
Matthew 6:6-8; Philippians 4:6-7
In the "America's Next Best Friend" reality show, kids see God will always be their one, true friend.........................34

Don't Push My Buttons *Proverbs 4:10-11; 29:17; Luke 2:51-52;*
Colossians 3:20; Ephesians 6:1-3
Students learn the art of debate as they perform an exchange between kids and parents 38

I Don't Know, but I've Been Told *Isaiah 1:1-4, 11-20*
Teens learn God cannot tolerate sin in this silly reenactment of a marching Marine Corps 42

Dear Jeremiah *Jeremiah 1:4-10; 20:7-11; 23:28-29*
Aware God knew them before they were born, students write letters sent to them by God 46

Fraud Buster, Private Eye *Jeremiah 14:14; 22:3; 23:2; 26: 28:15*
Fraud Buster must find the authentic bills as students learn the Bible is a truth detector 50

Danny Dawg and the Master G *Daniel 1:8-17*
Teens perform a rap depicting the first chapter of Daniel 54

Casino Babylon *Daniel 5:1-18, 20, 21d-31*
A group of gamblers play a serious game of life and death in this morality skit 58

A Tale of Five Piggies *Hosea 14:1-7*
Pig characters track through the dirt—only to find out that they're not happy in the mud 62

Let's Put It on the Calendar *Zechariah 6:12-13; 9:9; 11:12-13; 12:10; 14:3-4*
In a radio panel interview format, students discover the mysteries of Old Testament prophecy 66

Hope in the Hallway *Malachi 1:1, 5, 11; 2:8; 3:1-4*
Just like the children of Israel, three students face discipline for their foolish actions 70

Where's Your Pride? *Matthew 7:7-11; Hebrews 12:5b-10; Proverbs 18:24*
A pride of lions learns God uses families to teach character, wisdom, and discipline....................................74

Time Waster and the Triangle Test *Acts 8:26-31, 34-35; 17:1-3; 1 Peter 5:12-14; 2 John 1*
In an old-school radio melodrama style, students portray the lesson of Time Waster. 78

Mapping Out a Mission *Acts 16:6-15*
Using a paper floor map, two characters survive a journey and bring others on the road to Christ 82

The Secret Life of Crimson la Rouge *Acts 21:10-14, 27-28, 31, 33; 23:11*
Crimson la Rouge always thought being red would be easy;
a metaphor about the costs of following Christ 86

From Bug to Beauty *Acts 9:15, 19b-22; 22:5b-15*
Monarch—a butterfly with an attitude—becomes a metaphor for God's transforming power......................90

Who Needs a Pinky Toe? *1 Corinthians 12:14-27*
In this spiritual allegory, human body parts argue over their importance 94

Sock It to Ya *Galatians 2:11-14; 2 Peter 3:15-16*
A sock puppet show demonstrating the truth spoken in love doesn't equal angry criticism 98

Looking for Mr. J *1 Thessalonians 4:14-17; Titus 2:11-14*
Preparations for a special visitor reveal the parallel with Christ's return 102

Givers and Takers *2 Timothy 4:9, 13; Philippians 2:19-25; 4:18*
Alternating between pantomime and action, genuine acts of love and mere words are contrasted 106

Topic Index..110
Scripture Index...111
Bible-in-Life Correlation Chart 112

Introduction

For adolescents, performance is part of life. Their world is a stage, full of characters—both good and bad—who chase dreams, make judgments, search for answers, and long to know God more intimately. The theater is not just for the dramatic few. It offers a chance for young people to perform in a safe environment, giving each one a chance to become someone else if only for an afternoon.

Action! Cool Theater is chock full of active, imaginative explorations of Bible truths. Most require only a few props and a simple set. Get ready to teach your students by starting with the Bible Background at the beginning of each lesson, and ask what God wants to teach you personally. Then turn the page for some easy Helps and Hints for Middle Schoolers to enrich learning and a simple list of props and costumes.

You'll find two kinds of dramas in this book: scripts to read and improvisational activities that require quick thinking and creativity. The scripts make great readers' theater events, or the kids can rehearse, memorize lines, and stage full productions. The improvisational activities challenge kids to think on their feet and get them connected to each other in new ways. This collection uses contemporary genres like reality television, rap, and game shows, while also borrowing some old-school tricks like radio dramas, detective stories, puppet shows, and allegories. Creative, practical, modern, and insightful—these short plays offer unique insights into the biblical principles that influence our Christian walk. Universal themes such as obedience, friendship, and prayer are put in modern situations so young people can actively examine the choices they face every day. At the end of each script or activity, you'll find Curtain Call discussion questions that will help students apply the Bible truth. The discussion doesn't have to take a long time, but a few minutes focused on learning will reap great rewards.

How to Use This Book

You can use the activities and scripts in any order. Adapt them to your available space and time. These dramatic activities can be a supplement to David C. Cook's *Bible-in-Life* or *Echoes* curriculum—or any curriculum, for that matter. You can also find the right activity for your class using the Topic Index or Scripture Index at the back of the book. You'll find the Bible Background at the start of each script or activity. Match up an activity to a Bible story you're studying with your students, and let the drama add excitement to your learning time.

You can also use a script or activity as the core of your learning time. Take a few minutes to look up the Bible story and review it together. Then follow the simple directions for the script or activity to explore the Bible truth the story teaches. Then wrap up with the discussion questions.

Taking the Stage

As the director, stage manager, and master of ceremonies for your class, keep in mind the following suggestions.

Drama and dramatic exploration call for laying aside inhibitions, taking risks, and being comfortable performing in front of a group. Naturally some students will have more aptitude for this than others. It's important to establish a positive, safe, and encouraging atmosphere. Let students know up front that you will not tolerate teasing, put-downs, or negative comments. Take it one step further and ask students to affirm and encourage one another following each activity.

Emphasize the importance of the students being a good audience for one another. Students will be tempted to plan their own presentation or whisper last-minute ideas to their group members while in the audience. Require undivided attention to the performers, with no comment or movement from the audience.

Many of the activities are just that—active. Some of the games are by nature loud and rowdy. Many times students will be working in small groups in various parts of the room or building. You will find it extremely helpful to establish signals with your students, such as a clap or whistle—a signal for when you need silence, a signal for everyone to freeze, and a signal for when it's time to gather back together. Bring in a special bell, gong, or other noisemaker if you like. This will add humor, save your voice, and spare you potential frustration.

While this book is designed to blend seamlessly into the *Bible-in-Life* curriculum, any group can perform these short plays. Each performance script is inspired by Scripture and includes biblical background and hints for working with adolescents. Since none of the plays requires elaborate costumes or sets, these can be done in homes, classrooms, on simple stages, or in gymnasiums.

So what are you waiting for? Let's see what creativity you can coax out of hiding. Gather your performers, assign roles, and get ready to pull the curtain. *Ready, set, action!*

Patrick the Powerful and the Kid Kingdom

Bible Basis:

1 Samuel 8:4–10, 19–22

Memory Verse:

Trust in the LORD with all your heart and lean not on your own understanding; in all your ways acknowledge him, and he will make your paths straight.
Proverbs 3:5–6

Bible Background

Ah, the Israelites. A nation of sometimes lovable, often stubborn, all-too-human folks who just couldn't get it together on most days. Sound familiar?

After following a theocratic system of government where God directed all of their rules through prophets and priests, Israel wanted a change. They had entered and conquered most of the land promised to them by God through Abraham. But soon the nation was seduced by the cultures and religions of the people among whom they lived.

So now the Israelites were restless. The last verse of Judges says it best: "In those days Israel had no king; everyone did as he saw fit" (Judg. 21:25). Even though they were rejecting God's ultimate lordship over them, Israel asked for a king, and God granted their request.

Samuel was Israel's faithful prophet, judge, counselor, and priest at this time. He was actually one of the most effective prophets the nation had experienced, but they still wanted to try their own idea. Talk about stubborn!

God knew if these obstinate people had a king, they would quickly forget that their true leader was God. The Israelites had their eyes on material and political growth and power, and they kept ignoring the truth that spiritual strength was what they most needed.

Despite the poor choice they were making, God allowed His people to have their way. It was the only way they would learn.

Summary

In this short skit, the story of the Israelites rejecting God's leadership is paralleled in a modern version set in a middle school science classroom. A group of students revolt against their teacher, deciding to put one of their own in charge. In a not-so-surprising turn of events, the students find that their "kid kingdom" is a disaster in every sense.

Setting

A middle school classroom

Props

★ A stack of folders/papers, etc.
★ A set of keys
★ Chairs, set up in classroom style
★ Fire extinguisher
★ *Optional*: science props like test tubes, rubber tubing, safety goggles

Cast of Characters

★ Patrick
★ Patrick's three assistants
★ Mr. Imincharge (the teacher)
★ Sarah Whiny
★ Ima Complainer
★ Discontented Doug

Helps and Hints for Middle Schoolers

The idea of authority—and its boundaries—is particularly relevant for middle school kids who are trying to figure out how much control they have over their changing lives. When middle schoolers complain about those in authority over them, encourage them to find some creative solutions to the conflict instead of moaning and possibly rebelling. Realize that students' parents will have varying parenting styles; they will each have different rules and means for enforcing them. Rather than getting into a comparison contest of authority styles, draw out teens' ideas about authority—who they respect and why.

Patrick the Powerful and the Kid Kingdom

*(As the scene begins, the kids talk among themselves while their teacher, **Mr. Imincharge**, is out of the room.)*

Sarah: Don't you think Mr. Imincharge is too strict? He makes us clean up the lab after every experiment, and we have to follow every little instruction. It's crazy.

Doug: Yeah. Last week he made me wear safety goggles for no reason. I've even seen him make kids wipe down the counters three times before he would let them go to lunch.

Ima: If you ask me, I think we could run this class ourselves. Who needs a teacher anyway?

Doug: Why don't we elect our own leader and just get rid of Mr. Imincharge?

Sarah: But who could we pick as our leader?

*(The kids begin to talk together quietly while **Patrick**, a strong-willed and charismatic student, strides into the classroom. He is flanked by three friends who strut in beside him with arms crossed.)*

Patrick: *(arrogantly)* Hello, my fellow scientists and brilliant peers. I know you all missed me, but I was working on my plot to take over the world. I suppose we can start now that I've arrived. *(Looks around the room.)* Make room for my assistants.

*(The newcomers settle into chairs as **Mr. Imincharge** enters.)*

Mr. Imincharge: Okay, let's get started. Today's experiment is pretty dangerous, so pay close attention as I lead you through every step.

*(**Mr. Imincharge** starts to set up an imaginary experiment at the front of the class. The kids snicker and look around at each other. Finally, **Ima** speaks up.)*

Ima: Excuse me, but we've been having a class meeting, and we have another idea.

Mr. Imincharge: Excuse me?

Sarah: That's right. We've decided we don't need you to teach us. *(She gestures toward **Patrick**.)* Patrick is smart enough to run the classroom.

Patrick: *(looking surprised, but pleased)* Uh, that's . . . that's right! My buddies and I are totally capable of taking charge of this experiment. Who's more "intelligenterous" than me? *(He looks around for approval.)*

Doug: I say we take a vote!

All kids: *(chiming in)* Yeah, yeah, let's vote! A vote's the right thing to do! I'm ready! Let's vote!

*(The kids huddle together for a minute, whispering, while **Mr. Imincharge** looks on, looking mildly amused.)*

Patrick: Okay, Mr. I. You're out and I'm in!

(Kids cheer.)

Mr. Imincharge: I see. Well, I think you're making a big mistake. Today's experiment isn't as easy as it looks. But if you really want Patrick to be in charge, I'll give him the keys to the classroom. I'll let you do what you want this time.

(Mr. Imincharge hands Patrick a stack of folders and the keys. As he walks out, he stops to gaze over at the classroom and shakes his head.)

Patrick: Hooray for the Kid Kingdom! We're in charge for once! *(Everyone cheers.)*

Sarah: So what should we do first?

Patrick: Let's just have fun doing this experiment. Here, Doug, take this lighter. Ima, grab those chemicals over there. I need the three of you to spread out that big sheet. . . .

(Patrick begins to arrange an imaginary experiment, and the room is soon in chaos. The assistants chase each other. Doug tries to light his hair on fire. The girls do their nails and text on cell phones. Suddenly, Patrick makes a frightened announcement.)

Patrick: *(loudly, over the chaos)* Hey, ah, you won't believe this, but . . . THE CLASSROOM'S ON FIRE!

(The entire group erupts in fear and confusion; everyone charges the door. Kids scream FIRE! and HELP! as they run away.)

(Mr. Imincharge runs in with the fire extinguisher and acts as if he's putting out a fire. He then looks at the extinguisher as if checking the gauge and shakes his head.)

Mr. Imincharge: Why don't they ever listen? That's the fourth fire extinguisher I've gone through this year. "Intelligenterous"—right. Following the real leader is one lesson they never seem to learn. *(Mutters as he leaves)* Guess it's time to raise the old fire insurance again. . . .

Curtain Call

After the skit, discuss how it reflects Israel's discontent with God's system and their desire for a human leader.

★ **Why would students think they were a better choice than a teacher to run a classroom?** *(inflated view of themselves, rebellious toward authority, personality conflict with the teacher, etc.)*

★ **Can you think of some real-life examples when people demanded to run things themselves?** *(Students might point out situations in other parts of the world, historical situations, or local scenarios.)* **What happened as a result?** *(Try to bring out the unfortunate or catastrophic results, if possible.)*

★ **For both the fictitious students in the skit and the real-life Israelites, what was the real problem?** *(Our sinful natures want to rebel against God, which leads to pride, disobedience, rebelling against those in authority over them, etc.)*

★ **Can you think of a time when you wanted to do things your own way instead of God's way?** *(Encourage open sharing and discussion.)*

★ **What happens when we try to take over instead of responding positively to the authorities in our lives?** *(We can make major mistakes, suffer bad consequences, end up in a worse situation, lose people and things that matter to us, and lose touch with God.)*

Light Fraud Speaks Out

Bible Basis:

1 Samuel 28:1a, 3–19

Memory Verse:

Dear friends, do not believe every
spirit, but test the spirits to see
whether they are from God,
because many false prophets have
gone out into the world.
1 John 4:1

Bible Background

Who doesn't wish they had a little magic sometimes? A crystal ball, a fortune-teller, a consultation
with a ghost or two—it's just fun and games, right?

In 1 Samuel 28, the Israelites had once again proven their humanity by allowing witchcraft and
divination to seep into their culture despite clear warnings from God. King Saul had expelled those
who practiced such things, yet because of his impatience with God's own signs and powers, Saul
consulted the witch of Endor—a spiritual medium outside of town. Perhaps Saul had banned
mediums and wizards in an outward display of obedience, but in his heart, he hadn't given up the
practice of occult involvement "just in case."

Saul is like many of us who say we don't want anything to do with evil or occult activity. But
when a situation gets desperate or we don't get the results from God that we hoped for, the occult
can draw us in if we haven't determined in our hearts that it's totally off limits.

Saul's decision to take the occult route would prove deadly. He had lost God's blessing already
because he had disobeyed God's clear instructions. His choice to dabble in darkness would soon
bring him deep pain because God would execute judgment for his disobedience. Saul's epitaph
in 1 Chronicles 10:13–14 states that his death was a punishment by God for his continued
disobedience.

Summary

A character named *Light Fraud* speaks so-called "truth" to his audience, but is really darkness in disguise. His monologue about darkness and light gives insight into the dangers of occult practices.

Setting

A modern stage

Props

★ A white sheet or all-white clothing

Main Character

★ Light Fraud is a seemingly charming and charismatic character. He can be played by either a man or woman, but should be dressed in white with a well-groomed and rosy-cheeked demeanor.

★ His purpose is simple: to make darkness appear bright and harmless. Like the character of Screwtape in C.S. Lewis's classic story, *The Screwtape Letters*, Light Fraud is well aware of the naïveté of his audience.

Helps and Hints for Middle Schoolers

Middle schoolers can be clueless about the reality of evil and Satan's power. They can easily confuse the truth about Satan with what is presented in fantasy novels, movies, and video games. Be intentional and clear about separating the truth of Satan's schemes from fiction and imaginative fantasy.

Approach this topic soberly, not wanting to scare students, but impressing on them that fooling around with the occult is truly dangerous. Welcome their questions and conversation so you can help them recognize faulty beliefs and unnecessary fears.

Emphasize the power and presence of God. Don't start living in fear of Satan—we have God's protection.

Note: It is very important to discuss this performance with your group immediately afterward. Although the monologue is clearly ironic, some young people may need help deciphering the manipulative tools of such a deceptive character.

Light Fraud Speaks Out

Unlike some of the lighter dramas in this collection, Light Fraud Speaks Out *confronts a serious subject. It might be best to have an adult perform this monologue—especially since it involves delicate issues of witchcraft and sorcery.*

During this monologue, the main character must balance a cheerful exterior against his sinister purpose. As the monologue progresses, the actor might want to reveal clues about his real nature—maybe a slip of black under the white garments, or having the lights dim gradually during the performance. He's dressed in white (perhaps even a simple sheet), and as he first enters the room, he's surprised to see the audience.

Oh, pardon me. I didn't expect so many of you to be here when I arrived. I was hoping for one or two, but this is great! How are you? *(begins to shake hands with random people).* Aren't you a cutie! And look at you, too. I'm sure you are your mother's favorite child—so strong and handsome.

I suppose I should tell you the reason I came here. I am, you see, a bit unusual. I am neither human nor spirit, but I've come to tell you about some thrilling, adventurous, and completely secret opportunities. You are definitely the lucky ones, but you mustn't tell your parents about it. And definitely don't say a word to your youth leaders at church. They're . . . *(makes a "crazy" gesture around his head)* . . . oh, you know.

My name is Light Fraud. I was named for the bright message I have to share. *(lowers voice and comments to the front row)* Don't worry about my last name—it's got no significance whatsoever.

Have you ever wished you could perform magic? Or maybe you've wished you could see into the future. Some of you might think it would be *so cool* to talk to a ghost. Palm reading and tarot cards are really awesome too. Honestly, they're just fascinating little games to experiment with on the weekend when you and your friends want a little excitement.

Some people might have told you that these things are risky—maybe even dangerous. I'm here to tell you that these activities can unlock secrets that only you can discover. How does that sound? Are you curious? You could tap into all the things you've read about in fantasy books or seen in movies. Yes, you! Just think! You could cast spells, get advice from the dead. Maybe even concoct a little curse or two on those classmates who can be so annoying sometimes.

The spirit world is an exciting place of adventure and opportunity. If you and your friends want to dabble in it, what harm could there be? In fact, you can become smarter, more popular, and infinitely more powerful if you'd just loosen those restrictions adults place on you and explore my territory. Who's to say no?

(voice growing more eerie, less bright) How do you get started, you ask? Well, get some books about witchcraft and read all you can about it. You're at the perfect age to learn about sorcery, and divination, and channeling. Hey, why not learn all you can about the ancient wisdom! That's all it is really—learning how to direct your power as the druids did. I'd also recommend some tarot cards, and a magic board, or some crystals from the neighborhood magic shop. *(in a stage whisper)* Your parents probably won't understand, so keep it to yourself. They think they need to protect you, but we all know you can handle it.

I have lots of friends, so keep an eye out for other kids who know all this cool, dark stuff. It can feel so good to belong to such an undercover group. Your circle of friends will lead you even deeper into the mysteries of the universe. . . . God won't mind. The Bible only warns against *black* magic. This isn't evil or anything. Remember the witches in *The Wizard of Oz?* You could be like the Good Witch . . . or it might be more fun to be the Wicked Witch. You get to decide.

(Growing even more creepy) In fact, I'm on my way to meet a couple of friends just now, and I'd love for you to come. *(gestures to the audience to follow him)* C'mon—I know you'll like them. They know how to have a really good time. Let's go now . . . it's almost time for our gathering . . . I know you'll like it . . . you'll see . . .

Light Fraud *slinks out of the room, trying to entice his audience until the very end.*

Curtain Call

★ **What kinds of vibes or feelings did this character give you?** *(Weird, scary, strange, eerie. Some young people who are possibly toying with the occult might have found the character appealing or interesting.)*

★ **How did this monologue clue you in to Satan's strategies?** *(rationalizing involvement in dark things by saying it would make you popular, giving the impression it's harmless, saying it's cool, secret, and powerful, using peer appeal and curiosity as logical reasons to dabble in it, downplaying the dangers, encouraging deception of parents and other caring adults, etc.)*

★ **Why is the occult so dangerous?** *(It can seem innocent and harmless, but because demons are real, you can get in way over your head very quickly. Playing with things that Satan controls is always high risk. Engaging anything of the occult is giving Satan an opening into your life and heart.)*

★ **What do you do if you or a friend has already been experimenting with occult activities?** *(Quit right now! Show your friend where the Bible explains how harmful and wrong the occult is and how it is completely against God. Confess your actions and desire for occult involvement to God and let Him be your shield against Satan's schemes. Know and trust that God's power is much stronger than Satan's, and when you acknowledge God, Satan has no hold on you!)*

Wisdom Walks the Red Carpet

Bible Basis:

1 Kings 3:5–14

Memory Verse:

If any of you lacks wisdom,
he should ask God, who gives
generously to all without finding fault,
and it will be given to him.
James 1:5

Bible Background

Wisdom is the ability to discern what is best over what is simply good, and strength of character to act on that knowledge.

Solomon had a short wish list. He asked only for "a discerning heart." Solomon already had a degree of wisdom that prompted him to ask God for even more of it. He realized that wisdom would profit him much more than money and power.

Solomon has few rivals in Old Testament history. His extraordinary life of power and prosperity was only trumped by his reputation for wisdom. First Kings 10:24 says "the whole world sought audience with Solomon to hear the wisdom God had put in his heart." He was a scientist, writer, king, and military strategist who built an empire through peaceful commerce.

Because Solomon was so successful from a material and earthly perspective, his request of the Lord for wisdom above all else is a powerful lesson. Who among us wouldn't want the discernment of Solomon? Solomon's example helps us see what God values: inner character more than outward manifestation of spirituality. Solomon would have been even wiser if he had kept his commitment to God. His downfall shines light on the reality that having wisdom isn't the main thing; it's what you do with it.

God invites us in James 1:5 to ask for wisdom in the same way Solomon asked. Asking to be wise is the first step; then we have to ask God for the single-mindedness to use that wisdom and follow through with wise choices. God may not bless us with huge riches—though He can if He chooses to—but He will give us the blessings of using godly wisdom well, and those blessings are enormously more valuable than money and what it can buy.

Summary

Small groups will film short plays illustrating the principle found in a key verse from Proverbs. Many of your students have technical expertise with video editing. This project can be as elaborate or simple as your group desires. You may decide to allow several sessions for students to develop their film projects, then schedule an evening for the "premieres" of their work, complete with a red carpet, film critics, and awards.

Setting

Students' choice

Props/Materials

★ Video cameras, digital cameras with video capability, camera phones, computers with cameras, etc.: one per group of three to four students, Bibles
★ Various prop possibilities (costumes, gadgets, etc.)
★ A large screen television with appropriate cable connections to view the film festival entries
★ Red carpet for nominees and awards (*optional*)

Helps and Hints for Middle Schoolers

Adolescents love independence and action, but their judgment is still childlike in many ways. During an independent activity such as filmmaking, give your kids appropriate guidelines and observe from a distance as they work. Step in only if you see escalating conflict, indecision, or inappropriate behavior. They will appreciate the opportunity to be creative with their friends while learning. The activity also offers a chance for young teens to learn collaborative work. When appropriate, compliment various students for their initiative, creativity, interpersonal skills, etc.

Procedure

Groups will create original characters and a script for a performance of no more than five minutes. Each group can choose a narrator for voice-overs, or film live dialogue.

Groups can depict a verse literally—such as pretending to be ants preparing for winter or filming a nagging wife who is like a dripping faucet—or act out a scene that demonstrates a Proverbs principle, such as a situation when someone's temper leads to disaster.

Walk students through basic steps to accomplish their assignment. Suggest groups divide the tasks of scripting, set preparation, filming, and editing. Allow time for acting practice, but stay out of their way so the production is their own.

Groups can choose one of the following themes from the book of Proverbs, using one of the suggested passages or one they've chosen on their own.

The sluggard v. the hard worker: Proverbs 6:6–11; 13:4; 14:23; 20:4

Gossip: Proverbs 11:12–13; 16:28; 20:19

Friendship: Proverbs 12:26; 17:17; 18:24

Anger: Proverbs 12:16–18; 15:1, 18; 16:32

The family: Proverbs 1:8–9; 13:1, 24; 17:6

Our reputation: Proverbs 22:1

Curtain Call

The book of Proverbs is like a huge collection of good ideas from a very wise guy. Solomon tackles real-life experiences we all have. What do you think about Solomon's ideas in your group's Proverbs passage? *(Students will have various ideas.)*

★ How practical do you think your verse is for everyday life? *(Very practical, it fits with everyday life situations. Students may have a variety of thoughts, so encourage them to explain how they reached their conclusions.)*

★ How easy or hard do you think it would be to change a habit or behavior in order to follow the wise course in the verse you acted out? Why? *(might be hard because it means changing a habit you've had a long time, have to stop doing things friends do, changing is hard, it might be wrong to do something like gossip, but maybe we don't really want to change)*

★ Why does it matter whether you control your temper or keep from gossiping and treat your friends with respect? *(How you act shows what's in your heart. Your actions show people what you value and believe. If you're really a Christian, it should be obvious in the way you act.)*

★ What rewards could there be for choosing to do what's wise, like caring about having a good reputation, or making a strong effort to control anger? *(You could get along better with people, have more friends, not get in trouble as much, feel better about yourself, please God, and become more like Jesus.)*

If any of you lacks wisdom,
he should ask God, who gives generously
to all without finding fault,
and it will be given to him.
James 1:5

The Advice Is Right

Bible Basis:

1 Kings 12:3-16

Memory Verse:

Listen to advice and accept
instruction, and in the end
you will be wise.
Proverbs 19:20

Bible Background

Whether it's a car repair or marriage counsel, there's no shortage of people ready to give their advice. But who do you trust? Looking for advice is wise, but choosing your advisors takes the most wisdom of all.

Rehoboam, Solomon's son, inherited the throne in Israel when Solomon died. His reign started off rocky—and went down from there. Soon after Rehoboam was crowned, he found himself facing a disgruntled kingdom. The Israelites were angry about the years of heavy taxation and military burdens Solomon had imposed. The people saw the change in leadership as an opportunity for a change for the better. They presented their case to Rehoboam, who then looked for some quick advice. He consulted two groups: the older men who had been Solomon's advisors, and guys his own age he had grown up with. He got two totally different suggestions. Now what?

Rehoboam didn't appear to evaluate the information he'd collected. He chose to take the advice of his young, inexperienced peers, ignoring the compassionate counsel of the men who had experience in ruling a nation. The younger guys' unqualified and rash suggestions for how to deal with the people resulted in the division of Israel. Some left to the north, leaving Rehoboam to rule Judah, the southern tribes of Israel.

Rehoboam didn't have the wisdom of his renowned father, and didn't ask God to give him the wisdom he lacked. He failed to listen to wise advisors as well. The results were disastrous, for him and for the entire country.

Summary

In the game show, *The Advice Is Right,* contestants win prizes by asking their phone-a-friend for advice. The winner discovers the importance of choosing one's advisors carefully.

Setting

Modern

Props

★ A long table for contestants to stand behind
★ Game show-style music (if available)
★ Clock to tick off (or someone doing sound effects)
★ Prop microphone
★ A cell phone or old phone receiver
★ Buzzers: 3 drinking glasses and 3 metal spoons. Each contestant has one glass and one spoon. To "ring the buzzer," the player taps the glass with the spoon.

Cast of Characters

★ Rob Sparker, television host
★ Ms. Mandy Screecher, contestant (high strung, unreasonable, and foolish)
★ Mr. Will Listen, contestant (listens carefully to all sides—uses logic and common sense)
★ Mr. Ivan Knowzit, contestant (doesn't listen to advice at all—goes out on his own)
★ Four offstage phone voices (Eric, Ted, Jocelyn, and Jenny)
★ Runner to bring in results

Helps and Hints for Middle Schoolers

Adolescents are generally eager to follow the input from their inexperienced peers over the more "old-fashioned" viewpoints of parents or other wise adults. The lesson from 1 Kings about Rehoboam's foolish choices is particularly applicable for this age group. Avoid talking negatively about peers' advice. Instead, work to guide students toward a realization about where wise advice can be found. Encourage dialogue between students; ask them to share a time when they had an experience like Rehoboam's. Let them brainstorm wise sources of advice.

The Advice Is Right

Three contestants stand behind a long table holding three "buzzers" and a telephone. Off-stage, an announcer introduces television host **Rob Sparker**. *Everyone applauds.*

Sparker: Welcome, welcome to *The Advice Is Right* where contestants must make the right decision with a little help from their friends. Let's meet our contestants. (*Mandy Screecher is already screeching with excitement.*) Our first contestant is from High Pitch, Florida. Welcome, Ms. Mandy Screecher!

Screecher: (*with obnoxious enthusiasm*) Oh, Rob, I am just SO excited to be on your show. I've been watching you since I was 10 years old, and I'm ready to win some fabulous prizes because I lost all my treasured belongings in a tragic rhino assault in 1998, and . . . (*Sparker cuts her off.*)

Sparker: Thank you, Mandy, thank you so much. Our next contestant is a Mr. Will Listen from Wisdom Hill, Texas. How are you, Will?

Listen: Just fine, Rob. Thanks for having me.

Sparker: Next is a Mr. Ivan Knowzit, all the way from Smugville, Canada. Ivan, welcome! Is Smugville the real name of your city?

Knowzit: (*smugly*) Of course! Smugville was actually formed in 1832 after the French invaded its boundaries during the battle of Bighead.

Sparker: Fascinating. (*pause*) Okay, here's the deal. Each of you has an important decision to make. Before you answer, you can call up to two phone-a-friends for advice. Once you've heard their suggestions, you need to make a final decision. Any questions? (*As Sparker talks, each contestant listens with his or her character's unique personality: Mandy jumps up and down with excitement, Will focuses intently, Ivan rolls his eyes.*)

Sparker: Ivan, you're first. A friend has just asked to copy your homework since she was too busy the night before to do it herself. What should you do?

Knowzit: I already know the answer to that one!

Sparker: Wait a minute. Don't you want to ask a phone-a-friend for some advice?

Knowzit: Are you kidding? I don't need anyone else's advice. Of *course,* I'd give her my homework! *Everyone* knows that I have the right answers every time.

Sparker: Okay. Thank you, Mr. Knowzit. Now, Will Listen, here's your question. Your parents have asked you to rake the leaves before next Saturday. They'll pay you 20 dollars. What should you do?

Listen: Hmm. (*looks thoughtfully*) It sounds easy, but… I'd like to hear some advice first. I'd like to call my eighth-grade buddy, Eric. (*Will dials.*)

Eric: (*voice offstage*) Hey, buddy, I've been listening to the show, and I've got the right answer for you. Just take your parents' money, and give 10 bucks to your little brother to do the job. You've made a 10-dollar profit, and didn't have to do a thing! Wahoo!

Listen: I'm not sure about your idea, Eric. I think I need more advice before I make my final decision. I want to call Ted, my baseball coach. (*Phone rings a second time.*)

Ted: (*voice offstage*) Will—do what your parents asked and earn the 20 dollars fair and square. And don't wait, do it today. You'll learn to work hard and get your parents' respect.

Listen: Wow, Ted, I don't know. Eric's idea sounds a lot easier. But I trust you, man. You've had more experience with things like this. I'm going to go with your answer.

Sparker: So that's your decision?

Listen: Yeah, that's my final answer.

Sparker: All right. Now let's talk to Mandy. *(She squeals.)*

Sparker: You've talked too long between classes, and are now tardy. What should you do?

Screecher: That's the perfect situation for me, Rob—that happened to me last week! I have so many friends to ask … let's go with Jocelyn. She's on my speed dial. *(Dials)*

Jocelyn: *(voice offstage)* Hey, girlfriend! I heard the question—and I hate to tell ya, but you gotta come clean with your teacher. Just tell her you blew it and take the consequences.

Screecher: Whoa. I don't like *that* idea. I'm gonna give Jenny a call. *(Dials)*

Jenny: *(voice offstage)* Hi sweetie pie! I've got the perfect solution for you. If I were you, I'd get right over to the school nurse. Tell her you're feeling sick. Nurses always fall for that one. Plus, our dumb school makes too big of a deal about tardies anyway.

Screecher: I love it! You're so smart, Jen-Jen. That's my answer, Rob.

Sparker: All right. We've got all your answers. Let's wait as the judges reach their final verdict. *(Clock ticks, then a "runner" comes in and hands Rob a slip of paper.)* It looks like the winner is . . . Will Listen! (**Will** *comes forward while audience applauds.* **Mr. Knowzit** *stomps his feet angrily, and* **Mandy** *starts to cry loudly.)*

Sparker: Tune in next time when we play another round of *The Advice Is Right*!

Curtain Call

Lead the discussion from the skit's situations to real-life scenarios requiring wisdom.

★ **Can you think of a situation you've been in that was like one of these characters' situations? Where did you go for advice?** *(Answers will vary.)*

★ **Why do you think Rehoboam chose to take his friends' advice instead of the older men's ideas?** *(because he liked what they said, he wanted to keep his friends, he knew them better, he wanted the easy way out, he liked the feeling of power over the nation, etc.)*

★ **What do you think are the basic differences between the advice of an older person and that of someone your own age?** *(Older people have more experiences that help them give better advice. They might have stronger faith and more Bible knowledge. Sometimes friends have better advice because they know you better. Younger people are more in tune with the world today.)*

★ **When you get two different kinds of advice about one problem, how do you decide which to follow?** *(You need to think about them both; don't decide too quickly. Ask a third person to see if they have an idea like one of the ones you already heard. Find out what God says about the subject. Think about what would happen if you follow one suggestion or the other.)*

★ **In what way could the Bible be useful when you need good advice?** *(It has lots of good advice. God's words can be trusted. God wants the best for us.)*

Worship Isn't for Spectators

Bible Basis:

2 Chronicles 5:12-13; Ezra 3:10-11;
1 Corinthians 14:15, 26-33

Memory Verse:

Shout for joy to the LORD, all the earth.
Worship the LORD with gladness;
come before him with joyful songs.
Psalm 100:1-2

Bible Background

If worship were only about swaying to a cool band, we'd have it easy. But the concept of worship in Scripture is associated with reverent fear, adoration, and wonder—not just carefree celebration.

The Old Testament concept of worship is varied. The patriarchs believed that God could be worshiped wherever He revealed himself; the temple later became a hub for worship rituals that included Scripture reading, exposition, prayer, and singing. Instruments and singing were significant elements in praising and giving thanks to God. In 2 Chronicles, when the musicians and singers offered praise to God in an orderly fashion, God's glory visibly filled their worship area. What an awesome experience!

Worship isn't just about watching worship leaders or listening to musicians performing. Scripture describes it as responsive; we hear God's Word and respond to it with our own voices of singing and praise. This interactive experience is what makes corporate worship so powerful and effective. We sense God and throw ourselves into honoring Him, and He is pleased by our communal efforts.

Paul outlines quite specifically in 1 Corinthians how worship involves all the church members as they speak, pray, sing, and preach according to the gifts the Holy Spirit has given them (see 1 Cor. 12). Both those leading worship and those in the congregation have integral parts.

Worship, as described in the Bible, was by no means subdued. Instruments and even shouting and dancing often accompanied worship. Jesus pointed out that worship is an expression of our love for God—not just an emotional reaction to music or performance.

Summary

Kids plan a *Creative Worship Festival*, using their gifts of songwriting, dance interpretation, poetry readings, artwork, and more—all designed to praise God through their diverse talents.

Setting

None

Props

★ Optional: Art supplies like markers, paper, scissors, glue

Cast of Characters

★ None

Helps and Hints for Middle Schoolers

Most of your young people will have a limited concept of worship. We tend to define it according to our individual church experiences, including the style of music shared and the formality or informality of the service. Introduce to young teens how their church experiences are probably a very narrow view of what it means to offer our gifts to God in praise and celebration.

Consider expanding teens' worship understanding by incorporating more worship in your meetings. Use readings, music, quiet meditation moments, exuberant celebration—as appropriate to your church body—to allow students to experience God and praise Him spontaneously and freely.

Be aware that many young people are attracted to more emotional styles of worship. This is fine, as long as they regularly remember to examine their motives in worship. Help them internalize the concept that when we come together to worship, it's all about God.

Procedure

1. Let your group know that they will be organizing a *Creative Worship Festival.* Make sure they realize that this is different from a talent show where the spotlight is on the performer. Instead, the focus should always be on honoring and glorifying God.

2. Share some ways in which God's people in both the Old and New Testaments offered praise to God:
   - ★ instrumental music
   - ★ vocal singing
   - ★ dance
   - ★ Scripture readings

3. Brainstorm with them some other creative ways that people can praise God using their talents:
   - ★ artwork
   - ★ music composition
   - ★ service projects
   - ★ creative writing

4. Allow students some freedom to design their own "offering." Set a time and date for sharing these offerings of worship in a corporate setting. *Note: Some churches may enjoy participating with the youth for this event, but be flexible. Kids who are focused on their own performance anxiety might be distracted from the higher purpose.*

5. Kids should never feel pressured to worship. Allow them to participate or simply observe. Either way, they will be impacted by the experience.

6. During the Festival, be sure to de-emphasize the performers themselves by limiting applause, announcements, and spotlights. Have kids pray both before and during the Festival that their hearts and those of the audience members would truly be focused on worshiping God. In this way, this event is quite different from the other performances in this collection.

Curtain Call

Expand students' thinking and personal application of worship with evaluation of their *Creative Worship Festival* and by sharing what they've discovered.

★ **What did you like best about the worship at our *Creative Worship Festival?*** *(Allow everyone to share as they desire. Offer your own affirming observations.)*

★ **What aspects of group worship did you find most meaningful and why?** *(Again, allow for input.)*

★ **How could you see changing our corporate worship experiences as a church or as a youth group to bring more authentic and meaningful worship?** *(Encourage creative ideas. Then bring them to your pastor or worship team. Perhaps this could be the start of a youth-led worship service at your church.)*

Shout for joy to the LORD, all the earth.
Worship the LORD with gladness;
come before him with joyful songs.
Psalm 100:1–2

Jumping Jehoshaphat

Bible Basis:

2 Chronicles 17:1–10

Memory Verse:

Go into all the world and preach
the good news to all creation.
Mark 16:15

Bible Background

In the long line of Old Testament kings, Jehoshaphat was counted among the best. His father, Asa, was a strong ruler who brought security and peace to Judah. As a child, Jehoshaphat must have witnessed his father's love of worship and his tough position against pagan idolatry. Jehoshaphat followed his father's earlier example as a God-fearing leader and his initial reign was blessed by God.

His kingdom enjoyed a peaceful time with neighboring enemies. Despite his political downfall after an ungodly alliance with wicked King Ahab, Jehoshaphat demonstrated a desire to spread the Word of God and His holy laws.

Three years into his reign, Jehoshaphat realized that his subjects were ignorant of God's laws. They didn't remember the stories of God's leadership and protection in Israel's earlier history and weren't able to live in a way that showed they honored God. So Jehoshaphat undertook a nation-wide religious education program. He sent some of his officials out to the land to teach the people, using God's Book of the Law as their manual.

What a wise move! Instructing the people at the basic level in what God's Word had said about following Him and honoring His covenant with them would give them the ability to live lives that pleased God and prospered the nation. As a sweet side effect, once the people began to grow in their devotion to God, neighboring pagan nations backed off because they could see how Judah was coming together around their common faith.

Summary

King J-Dogg, a godly ruler over the nation of Judah, shares his passion for teaching God's word throughout his kingdom. Either a student or adult actor can perform this modern, first-person monologue of King Jehoshaphat while the audience participates in the fun.

Since the urban slang is over-the-top, the main character can make this as exaggerated as he wants.

Setting

Modern stage

Main Character

★ King J-Dogg, based on Jehoshaphat, king of Judah
Note: Make sure this role is given to an actor who will handle it in a tasteful way and not in an offensive manner.

Props

★ A half-ancient, half-modern costume complete with robes, a crown, "bling" (gaudy necklace and rings), MP3 player, cell phone
★ A Bible

Helps and Hints for Middle Schoolers

Interpreting Old Testament history is easier for young people when it's translated into a modern context, such as this rapper skit. Whenever you can compare a biblical character or scenario to something contemporary that the students are familiar with, they'll catch on faster and see more personal relevance in the truth or teaching. When possible, find a way for students to connect their own lives or problems with those of the Bible character they're studying. In Jehoshaphat's case, consider the way he followed his father's example, his courage in dumping the idol remnants in Judah, and how he took action with a group of God-fearing guys to spread God's Word.

Jumping Jehoshaphat

King J-Dogg enters dressed in Old Testament robes and a crown, blended with hip-hop "bling" around his neck, an MP3 player, and a cell phone. He's confident, charismatic, and funny, and he knows how to hold his audience's attention.

Yo, yo, what up?

In case you're wondering where I got these crazy duds, I should tell you a little 'bout myself. I'm a king—King J-Dogg actually. If you think it's tough to run a country these days, you should see what I had to deal with in 874 B.C.!

Before I tell you about my land of Judah, you need to know a few things. If I say "God's Word," then you gotta do the wave, starting with this side on the right and ending on the other side. If I say "haters," then you need to give me a thumbs-down *(demonstrates)*. And when I say "King J-Dogg," you'll need to raise the roof—like this *(demonstrates with flat hands to the ceiling)*. Think you can handle it?

Like I said, my name's **King J-Dogg** *(waits for response)*. They used to call me Jehoshaphat, but no one knew how to spell it. Come to think of it, no one spells **J-Dogg** right either (it's got two g's), but that's beside the point.

Before I tell you about my country, you need to hear about my dad. He loved **God's Word** *(waits for audience to do the wave)*, and he knew how to keep it real. He was the king over Judah for 41 years, and he didn't fool around with the pagan religions or the God-**haters** *(waits for audience response)*. My dad worshiped God in every way, and I really wanted to follow in his footsteps.

Now I gotta admit. I love **God's Word** *(waits for response)*, and I'm spending a lotta time and bank spreading the good news. The **haters** *(waits for response)* from the countries next door don't mess with Judah. They know God is on our side, yeah, and we're getting stronger every day. **J-Dogg** *(waits for response)* ain't messin' with no idols and heathen shrines like some of the kings before me and my dad.

See this? *(holds up Bible)* This ain't just any book. It's the bona fide, authentic **Word of God** *(waits for response)*. This law is nonnegotiable and written in stone. As **king** *(waits for response)*, everyone in my land has to learn it, know it, and follow its commands. I've got me a group of guys to help teach this law in every city. They've got names like Ben-Hail, Obadiah, and Zechariah, or Z-Man, for short. In fact, stand up, guys. Yeah, you, and you, and you over there *(surprises three boys in the audience by asking them to stand)*. Let's put our hands together for these guys, preaching the good news *(wait for applause)*.

It's true, in my kingdom, you're either a God-**hater** *(waits for response)* or a God-lover. But even if you don't live in 874 B.C., you gotta make a choice. I'm asking you, are you spreadin' **God's Word** *(waits for response)*? Or are you hiding out in the shadows, hoping someone else will do the work? Man, if you're not in with me, sharing the **Word of God** *(waits for response)*, you be against me. That's deadly, man. I say we're in this together. Don't cut and run while your homies are carrying the load. Get out there with the **Word** *(waits for response)*. God's got you covered! Do it together, and stand strong with your buds.

Hey, I gotta run. My crew is waitin' for me back at the crib. **J-Dogg** *(waits for response)* here appreciates that you're helping out a brother by sharing the good news in the twenty-first century. Stay strong! Peace!

Curtain Call

Sharing God's Word with others is typically an uncomfortable idea. Diffuse some of the anxiety with a casual group discussion.

★ **Jehoshaphat followed his father's example as a strong believer in God. Whose example could you follow to be courageous and committed as Jehoshaphat was?** *(Students will have various responses.)*

★ **What roadblocks or issues keep you from telling your friends and others you meet about who God is and what you believe about Him?** *(fear, embarrassment, don't know how to do it or what to say, not cool, not good at talking to people, shy, etc.)*

★ **Jehoshaphat set himself up with other godly guys to get the Word out. How could you successfully hook up with other Christians to spread God's Word?** *(Start a Bible study or prayer group together. Do service projects as Christians to show what you believe. Join a campus Christian group. Get with a youth group that does evangelistic outreach and go out as a group to share about God.)*

★ **God honored Judah's devotion to Him by causing fear in the neighboring nations so they wouldn't attack Judah. Imagine what God could do if you chose to be serious and bold enough to tell others about God.** *(God could cause a revival in the church or school. Local government could be impacted to reflect Christian values. The school district could change policies to be more God-honoring, etc.)*

Go into all the world and preach the good news to all creation.
Mark 16:15

Courtly Courage

Bible Basis:

Esther 2:5-10; 3:1, 5-6, 13; 4:13-16

Memory Verse:

Be strong and courageous.
Do not be terrified; do not be
discouraged, for the LORD your God
will be with you wherever you go.
Joshua 1:9b

Bible Background

The book of Esther may not be the history lesson we expected. Would we have expected a book of the Bible to discuss women's beauty treatments, male chauvinism, pagan customs, genocide, a woman's boldness, or a polygamous king? The book of Esther also makes no direct references to God or prayer, although it does mention fasting, which is usually a time for prayer and seeking God. The book of Esther centers on events during the Persian exile when the Israelites were under the threat of genocide. Like much Old Testament history, it's not a very pretty story, but has drama and a miraculous ending.

Esther was another Jew whose life had been altered by the Babylonian victory over the Jews. Even after King Cyrus allowed the Jews to return to Israel, some Jews remained in what became Persia. Esther's family was among these. Persia was a world power at this point in history, and Esther came right into the eye of the hurricane by being chosen as King Xerxes' new wife.

Even as queen of Persia, Esther had few rights or freedoms. She was restricted by various Persian laws and customs. Her options were limited, but when the crunch came, Esther went for it. The question Mordecai asked of Esther—"Who knows but that you have come to royal position for such a time as this?" (Esth. 4:14)—suggests that God had placed this woman by divine appointment for a specific purpose. In this way, Esther's story reaffirms God's sovereignty in the affairs of humans.

Summary

With narrator-directed promptings, students perform an improvised version of the Esther story, using quick costume changes and props. It's a perfect activity for a larger group of students who might not be accomplished actors, but enjoy the energy of a fast-paced activity.

The director needs to be familiar with the story ahead of time. Also, give the narrator the script ahead of time. Enlist another stage manager or additional helper to keep the offstage chaos to a minimum and allow the plot to flow quickly from one scene to the next.

All the students can participate, if only as part of a crowd of Jews. Prepare actors by explaining that as the narrator reads, they'll have to listen carefully to rapidly figure out what to do. They should use pantomime while performing the plotline of Esther's story.

Setting

Imaginary court of King Xerxes in ancient Persia

Props

★ Two crowns
★ royal scepter
★ sign: "Men are in charge!"
★ sign: "Wipe out the Israelites!"
★ Random beauty supplies, like mirrors, hairspray, brushes, etc.
★ robe of honor

Cast of Characters

★ Narrator
★ King Xerxes—wearing a crown and royal robe
★ Queen Vashti—wearing a crown and royal robe
★ King's attendant
★ Two "bad guys" who are plotting to overthrow the King
★ Esther in queenly garb
★ Mordecai
★ Haman
★ Various groups, such as partygoers and miscellaneous young women

Helps and Hints for Middle Schoolers

This Biblical narrative has something for everyone, including two heroes. Esther and Mordecai both come out strong winners for their loyalty to their people and to God. Young people have an assortment of contemporary individuals they may call heroes. Help them contemplate and articulate what makes a hero. Prompt young teens to think beyond appearances and impressive yet superficial traits and abilities. Point to Esther and Mordecai as characters who exemplify heroism because they acted for principles and people outside themselves instead of to glorify themselves or impress others, as many modern "heroes" do. Encourage youth to consider potential role models who aren't in the spotlight but who mirror the honesty, humility, and sacrificial actions of the biblical characters. You might share a brief anecdote of a role model God has provided in your life and how that person influenced you positively.

Courtly Courage

The narrator should pause as needed to allow the actors to assemble themselves according to the suggested actions in the script. There are suggestions for each scene for the actors if they freeze, but allow them freedom to interpret the narrative as they choose.

Narrator's Script:

In the third year of King Xerxes' (*pronounced ZERK-sees*) reign, he decided to throw a huge party for his royal officials. He lavishly decorated and ordered expensive food for all the VIPs of the kingdom, who were invited. The party lasted a whole week, and the king was having the time of his life. (*King and party guests pantomime the party scene.*)

On the seventh day, King Xerxes called for an attendant to bring his wife, Queen Vashti, to join the festivities. He was hoping to impress everyone with her good looks since he had chosen the most beautiful woman to be his queen. But when the attendant ordered her into the presence of the guests, she refused! (*The attendant tries to get Queen Vashti to come, but she makes a scene and refuses.*)

The king, afraid of looking like a fool in front of his guests, lost his cool. The entire crowd feared that if the word got out that the queen could call the shots, men's authority everywhere would be threatened. So the king sent bulletins throughout his kingdom with this message: "Men are in charge!" (*King gets angry and has attendant post a sign on the wall: "Men are in charge!"*)

With the queen disgraced, the king's attendants started corralling all the pretty girls they could find. This harem of potential wives faced a series of beauty treatments as they competed for the attention of the king. The king looked forward to meeting the new girls. (*Girls assemble in front of mirrors, brushing their hair, putting on make-up, and primping.*)

One particular girl seemed to catch everyone's attention. She was the niece of Mordecai, an honest Jewish man. Her name was Esther, and the king's attendants gave her special treatment. (*Esther arrives; the other girls are obviously jealous. The king sees her and is smitten by her beauty. He puts a crown on her head.*) The king fell in love with her on the spot. He gave her a special place of honor and put the former queen's crown upon her head.

Now Esther had kept her Jewish heritage a secret as her uncle Mordecai had suggested. One day Mordecai overheard two of the king's advisors hatching a plot to overthrow the king. Mordecai spilled the news to Esther who shared it with her new husband, King Xerxes. (*Like the game of "telephone," the news moves along a line of characters: bad guys whisper, Mordecai hears, he tells Esther who tells the king.*)

King Xerxes was furious and ordered the execution of the two plotters. Shortly after, a man named Haman—one of his official's sons—gained the highest position in the land. Everyone bowed to him wherever he went. (*The king's attendant carries the bad guys offstage. Haman is promoted while various countrymen bow down to him.*)

But Mordecai would not bow to anyone. As a Jew, he saved his highest respect for God. Haman was furious about this and devised a way to eliminate the Jews altogether. Maybe he could wipe out all his enemies in a single swoop! (*Mordecai refuses to bow down to Haman. Angry Haman begins to hatch a sinister plot, possibly wringing his hands or with evil laughter?*)

Haman went to the king with his evil ideas. He convinced the king to completely wipe out the Jewish people from the land. The king gave Haman permission to send an official message to officials all over Persia demanding that Esther's people be massacred. *(Haman and the king chat. The king nods and Haman thumps a sign upon the wall: "Wipe out the Israelites!")*

Esther and Mordecai were devastated at this news. Esther knew that if her people were to be saved, she would have to act—even if it meant she might anger her husband, the king. She asked the Jews to fast and pray for her while she made her plan. *(Esther and Mordecai look distraught. The Jewish people—all the extra students—begin to pray.)*

In the next few days, Esther bravely approached the king with her request to save her people. The king discovered that his trusted assistant Haman was really a scoundrel, and a humble Jew named Mordecai was actually his ally. The king arranged for Haman to be hanged, and for Mordecai to be given honors. *(Esther approaches the king meekly, and he listens. Haman is dragged off by the attendant, and Mordecai is given a robe of honor.)*

In the end, the Jewish people were allowed to defend themselves against their enemies. God had used Queen Esther's courage to save the Jews! *(The Jewish people cheer and make victory signs, and Queen Esther is a hero!)*

Curtain Call

★ **What attitudes and characteristics did Esther show in this story?** *(courage, faith, caring for others ahead of herself, submission to authority, respect, etc.)*

★ **How would you define courage?** *(doing what's right despite the potential consequences, not showing fear, facing a hard situation, and not losing your head, etc.)*

★ **When have you personally witnessed an act of courage?** *(Let students share. Keep them on track and encourage brief answers so all who want to can speak.)*

★ **What are some reasons we might choose not to act with courage?** *(fear of something in the situation, fear of what others might say or do, uncertainty, not feeling capable or knowledgeable, our personal weaknesses or limitations, our social status, not being physically large or strong, lack of trust in God, lack of creative thinking, etc.)*

★ **How can we choose courage over being timid or fearful?** *(Watch for opportunities God brings and grab them. Be determined to be courageous so your first reaction is to act instead of to cave in. Don't second-guess or overanalyze. Hang out with the right people who will bolster your courage or stand with you. Trust in God's ability to stand up for you.)*

America's Next Best Friend

Bible Basis:

Psalms 34:17-18; 55:16-17;
1 Thessalonians 5:17;
Matthew 6:6-8; Philippians 4:6-7

Memory Verse:

Come near to God and
he will come near to you.
James 4:8a

Bible Background

Just when we wonder if we're the only one who feels giddy, devastated, passionate, or furious, we read the Psalms of David and realize that the human condition doesn't change from generation to generation.

Psalm 34 may have been written after the events of 1 Samuel 21, in which David feared Achish, King of Gath. His words give us assurance that God does indeed hear and respond to the prayers of the righteous. David's writing of Psalm 55 was prompted by Absalom's rebellion. David says he cried out to God morning, noon, and night—in other words, he kept calling out his complaints and moanings to God. Nothing says that God disliked this persistent prayer; in fact He responds to it, and even invites continual prayer, according to 1 Thessalonians 5:17. This continual prayer doesn't necessarily mean being in a physical attitude of prayer every minute of the day; it is rather a spiritual attitude of prayerfulness that underlies the rest of your activities and agenda.

That ongoing conversation with God throughout the day and night is a contrast to the prayer described in Matthew 6—intentional prayer that is the sole activity of the moment for the purpose of intense conversation with God. The Lord is most interested in the passion of our hearts and the sincerity of our prayers, not the stylish words or phrases that some people use when praying in public.

Finally, God desires that we pray about everything, not just when we need a miracle or when things are too hard for us. Paul says in Philippians that our prayers should be cushioned in thankfulness, and should take the place of worry.

All these prescriptions for prayer guide us toward a deeper friendship with God, in which talking to Him, involving Him in our lives, and letting Him in on the real feelings and needs of our hearts, are essential.

Summary

Three judges assess a pool of contestants competing for the role of "Best Friend." In a reality TV format, *America's Next Best Friend* reveals the truth about our intimate friendships and helps students realize that God will always be their one, true friend.

Setting

Television studio where contestants audition for a show

Props

★ Long table with three chairs for judges
★ A stand microphone (real or fake) for each contestant

Cast of Characters

Three judges
★ Pauline
★ Randall
★ Mr. S.

Three contestants
★ Gabriella
★ Rodney
★ Shawn
★ Offstage voices (can be played by the three contestants)

Helps and Hints for Middle Schoolers

Ever see a group of middle school students clustered in a group? It's no secret that they are driven by position and popularity and will often perform to a crowd in order to gain approval. Friendships are the lifeblood of this age group, yet preteens often don't think about why they choose the friends they do. They can be horribly alone and lost when a friendship dissolves or goes sour. Having God as a friend will sound outlandish or impossible to some, since God can't shop, cheer for a favored sports team with them, or laugh about teen topics. But as young teens are hurt, let down, or disappointed by friendships, they will be looking for One who doesn't desert them, turn on them, or move away. Learning to pray and talk to God conversationally and from their hearts is the best way to grow in a friendship with God. Make prayer a regular part of time with your students, aiming for authentic conversation, not formulaic or stylistic prayers. Through time and more frequent conversations with their Father in heaven, preteens will develop a friendship that will last a lifetime.

America's Next Best Friend

The three judges are seated behind a long table waiting for contestants to audition.

Pauline: *(looking at her watch)* It's already three o'clock. We gotta get these contestants out here so I can get to my spa appointment.

Mr. S.: What is taking so long? Don't the producers know we are busy? We don't have all day. We've gotta find three more kids to compete for *America's Next Best Friend* before tomorrow.

Randall: *(shouting toward backstage)* Let's get moving, people! Send in the first contestant!

*(**Rodney** walks in, stands before the standing microphone.)*

Rodney: Hey. My name's Rodney.

Mr. S.: Hello, Rodney. Tell us what makes you think you can be *America's Next Best Friend?*

Rodney: *(acting cool and smooth)* Well, dude. I'm the kind of friend who isn't afraid to get crazy. I'm the kind of guy who'll take risks, you know what I'm saying? As long as you've got me, you'll never be bored on a Saturday night. Plus, I'm a chick magnet. Girls go wild for guys like me.

Pauline: Well, uh…thank you, Rodney, but I don't think you're what we're looking for.

Randall: You're right on, Pauline. Rodney, you might be good for a few laughs, but in the end, I'm afraid you won't go the distance. Sorry, man.

*(**Rodney** struts off, muttering under his breath. The second contestant, **Gabriella**, walks up to the microphone.)*

Pauline: And what's your name?

Gabriella: My name is Gabriella—but my friends call me Gigi for short. I'm like SO excited to be here. I just know I could be *America's Next Best Friend*!

Mr. S.: Gigi, why don't you start by telling us something about yourself?

Gabriela: I really need a best friend. I like to do everything with my BFF . . . go to football games every week, hang out at lunch, wear the same outfit when we go shopping. If I'm not with my best friend every second, I don't feel complete.

Randall: Hey, girl. You are way off. Don't you think friends need some space?

Gabriella: Oh no! If you're best friends with someone, then it's sort of like you get to control each other. Otherwise, someone else might come in and threaten your friendship. When two people are friends, then no one else should get in the way—

Pauline: Whoa—wait a second! I hate to interrupt you, but true friends don't cling to each other. You seem really insecure, honey. You better work through some of your issues.

Gabriella: *(runs to **Pauline** and hugs her, getting hysterical)* Oh, please, please, don't cut me! I just can't LIVE without someone who can do everything with me. . . .

Mr. S.: Gabriella, you're not what we're looking for. Please leave before we have to call security.

*(**Gabriella** gives **Pauline** one more hug, then runs offstage.)*

Randall: Wow . . . that was weird! *(calls offstage)* Next!

Shawn: *(unenthusiastically)* Hey. What's up?

Randall: Hi, Shawn. What makes you right for *America's Next Best Friend*?

Shawn: First of all, I've got a million friends. I'll never get in your face or expect anything from you. I like playing video games and tossing around the football, We could hang out at the movies—whatever. Don't call me, though, if you've got any problems. I'm not into that.

Mr. S.: You mean if your friend's in trouble, you want to keep your distance?

Shawn: Yep, that heavy stuff isn't what I'm about. I just like chillin' and having a good time.

Pauline: Good gracious, Shawn. You definitely will not make it to the next round.

Shawn: Hey, whatever. I don't really care anyway. I just wanted to get on TV. *(exits)*

Mr. S.: Strike three. We're out.

Randall: I can't believe it's so hard to find *America's Next Best Friend*.

Pauline: Maybe our standards are just too high. Come on, let's quit for today. There's always tomorrow, and my spa appointment won't wait. *(She and **Randall** start to walk off.)*

Mr. S.: *(following them off)* For the first time, I'm actually worried about a show. *(sighs)* Maybe it's time I got out of the business. *(Lights dim)*

Offstage Voices:

"The LORD is my strength and my shield; my heart trusts in him, and I am helped. My heart leaps for joy and I will give thanks to him in song" (Psalm 28:7).

"I will listen to what God the LORD will say; he promises peace to his people" (Psalm 85:8a).

"O LORD, you have searched me and you know me. You know when I sit and when I rise; you perceive my thoughts from afar" (Psalm 139:1–2).

"Give thanks to the God of heaven. His love endures forever" (Psalm 136:26). *(Lights out)*

Curtain Call

Help your students continue thinking about friendship by having the following discussion.

★ **How is friendship with God like a friendship with someone your age?** *(Students will have varied responses; accept all reasonable input.)*

★ **What makes God the best kind of friend?** *(He will accept you even when you're down and not very lovable. He knows you better than your best friend and loves you even more. He won't reject you and doesn't get tired of hearing you talk to Him. God wants the best for you in every situation. God will stick with you all your life no matter where you are or what's going on in your life.)*

★ **What does prayer have to do with friendship with God?** *(Talking to God and telling Him what's on your mind and what's going on in your life is the way you build a friendship with Him. God will listen to all the things you want to tell Him—the good things, the miserable times, the sadness, the frustrations, the complaining.)*

★ **What ideas about prayer have you heard that can deepen or launch your friendship with God?** *(Students will have various responses.)*

Don't Push My Buttons

Bible Basis:

Proverbs 4:10–11; 29:17; Luke 2:51–52;
Colossians 3:20; Ephesians 6:1–3

Memory Verse:

Listen, my son, to your father's
instruction and do not forsake
your mother's teaching.
Proverbs 1:8

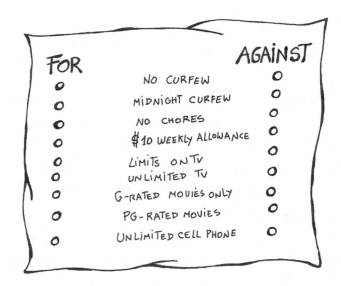

FOR | AGAINST
NO CURFEW
MIDNIGHT CURFEW
NO CHORES
$10 WEEKLY ALLOWANCE
LIMITS ON TV
UNLIMITED TV
G-RATED MOVIES ONLY
PG-RATED MOVIES
UNLIMITED CELL PHONE

Bible Background

Does the Bible give us practical advice—or simply historical truth? The answer is both. The book of Proverbs is eminently practical, offering us advice on everything from business management to family relationships. Solomon shared his God-given wisdom, often giving advice to children and their parents. He also promised that when children obey their parents and listen to their advice, a longer and more productive life would be the result.

The historical record can provide practical insight as well. Luke's account of Jesus at the age of 12 describes the time when Mary and Joseph were in Jerusalem for the Passover celebration. As an example to each of us, Scripture states that after this incident, Jesus went back to the small village where he had grown up and lived under his parents' authority.

Paul, like Solomon, gives God-inspired advice for living in harmony with one's family. In his letter to the Ephesians and again in Colossians, Paul instructs children to *honor* their parents—a word from the Greek that suggests an attitude of respect toward others worthy of value. Children who are obedient and respectful toward their parents will develop the ability to obey and respect other authorities they will encounter later in life. The home is the garden center where right behavior and character are cultivated and nurtured so the fruit can be experienced in the wider world later.

Summary

Your group will participate in an extemporaneous debate between "parents" and adolescents, discussing issues of independence, faith, and obedience.

Instead of performing a set script, your students will prepare their own debate. This requires some maturity and depth of thinking, so you will want to judge the readiness of your individual group to participate. If you have a large group—or if some of your kids might not want to join in—you can allow for a student audience to judge the effectiveness of both sides' arguments.

If you have a particularly goofy group—one that finds it hard to take things seriously—try a few strategies. Have kids dress up in suits and dresses like a formal debate *or* consider videotaping the debate.

Setting

Space set up for a debate

Props

★ Timer
★ Table and chairs
★ Optional: podium

Helps and Hints for Middle Schoolers

Obedience is not a topic most young teens will be keen to dwell on. Either they get it, and have learned to obey with good results (hopefully), or they're not there yet. Some preteens may have been obedient as youngsters, but then begin to test the limits of obedience again. Rather than get into a debate of your own with students about what is fair and not fair, direct students to God's Word as the moderator for their issues with parents. Let them try to discern what God says about obeying outwardly while rebelling inwardly, obeying partially, or flagrantly disobeying. Point out the rewards that come from obedience and the ugliness that results from disobedience.

You won't change your students' minds in the space of a class, but your directing their thinking can lead them to continued consideration of God's ways and rewards for obedience. And it always is helpful to affirm right behavior that you observe, in and out of the classroom.

Procedure

Invite students to brainstorm issues that create conflict between kids and parents. Write these on a whiteboard or sheet of butcher paper. Expect ideas like curfew, clothing, friends, media, grades, and family relationships.

Next, students will divide into two groups—one representing parents and the other representing students. *(Note: You might be short of volunteers to represent parents! If so, choose a few class leaders ahead of time who agree to join the "parent cause.")*

Choose three issues from the brainstorming. Allow groups 15 minutes to prepare their opening statement and arguments for each issue.

An example of an opening statement might sound like this: **"Since young people are in the process of becoming adults, we believe that children should be given a later curfew, little by little, so that by the time we're on our own we will be able to handle adult situations."**

Position groups opposite each other. Choose an adult debate moderator to keep things moving, or moderate the debate yourself. Read the debate rules aloud:

Everyone will be given equal opportunity to speak.
Show respect and courtesy to the person speaking.
Raise your hand if you'd like to respond to the dialogue.
No one may speak for longer than three minutes at one time.
The moderator reserves the right to redirect a question or stop the debate.

Here are some sample lead-in questions for your debate:
Moderator: The Parent Group will begin. Please read your opening statement.
Parent Group: (Reads opening statement.) (Set timer for 2 minutes.)
Moderator: Thank you, Parents. Would the Young Adult representatives please give their opening statement?
Young Adult Group: (Reads opening statement.) (Set timer for 2 minutes.)
Moderator: Thank you, students. Do the parents have anything to say about what you've just heard? Do you have any questions for the students?
(Set timer for 6 minutes total, then move to a new question.)

The debate should move back and forth, giving each side a chance to speak. When there is a lull in the arguments, feel free to move on to the second and third issue, following the same protocol.

When the debate is finished, ask each side to thank and compliment the opposite team for their job well done.

Curtain Call

Continue the discussion about obedience to parents. Let the discussion move spontaneously, as long as it's a constructive interchange of ideas and truth. Don't let the situation deteriorate into a gripe session.

★ **When kids and parents can't agree on a solution to a conflict, which side gets to make the final decision? Why?** *(Parents should be the final decision makers because God has given them authority over their children. Kids need to obey even if they don't like the guidelines, because their obedience is what counts most, not the details of the issue itself.)*

★ **Why do you think God explicitly instructs children to obey their parents?** *(Because parents are supposed to know what's best for their kids, even if the kids can't see it. God put parents in authority over kids as His representatives to teach them what's right, and to help them learn the right response to authority so they can learn obedience to other authority figures later in life. Parents have experience and wisdom kids don't have, so parents can project and teach kids through their obedience.)*

★ **What if parents are wrong? If they are, then why does God want us to obey them anyway?** *(God has told us to obey our parents even if we disagree with their rules or actions. We obey God by obeying our parents, and that's always right. Obedience shows respect for parents because of the authority God has given them. We should obey parents unless they expect us to do something that is clearly against what God says.)*

Listen, my son,
to your father's instruction
and do not forsake your mother's teaching.
Proverbs 1:8

I Don't Know, but I've Been Told

Bible Basis:

Isaiah 1:1–4, 11–20

Memory Verse:

Take your evil deeds out of my sight!
Stop doing wrong, learn to do right!
Isaiah 1:16b–17a

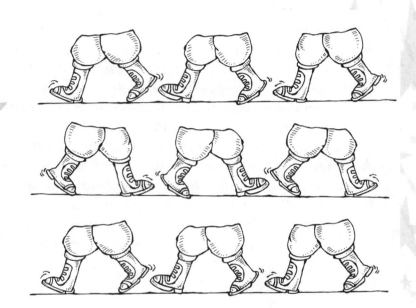

Bible Background

Straight talking. Visionary. Urgent. That's Isaiah, the greatest Old Testament prophet. He was called by God to expose the shameful rebellion of Israel as they broke their sacred covenant over and over again. Fake outward shows of obedience just wouldn't cut it, and Isaiah was not reticent in declaring God's judgment over their sin.

Isaiah is the first book written by the prophets in the Bible. Isaiah was well-liked initially, but like most other prophetic messengers, people soon became hardened to his messages of judgment for sin. Isaiah served as God's mouthpiece to Israel for 60 years, then was executed during the reign of King Manasseh.

As the book of Isaiah begins, the prophet is writing to Judah—the southern kingdom of the divided nation of Israel. Isaiah's name literally means "The Lord saves," and his urgent message to "rulers of Sodom" and "people of Gomorrah" was the pronouncement they needed to recognize their broken covenant. God directed Isaiah to blast the nation with the reality of their spiritual condition: They acted like they were godly, but their hearts were diseased with dishonesty and sin. Isaiah tried to reopen the Israelites' eyes to God's holiness and truth and love, but they defiantly and imprudently refused to pay attention. God truly wanted His people to repent and regain closeness with Him, but they just wouldn't listen. Anytime we refuse to hear what God is saying, we not only lose our connection with Him, but also risk His righteous and fearsome judgment.

Summary

Can you ignore directions without getting hurt? If you don't follow the rules, don't expect to be around for long. In this silly reenactment of a marching Marine Corps, kids will learn that God cannot tolerate sinful behavior.

Setting

Empty stage that is a Marine Corps drilling ground. The larger your group, the larger area you will need for this performance lesson.

Props

★ Military fatigues or camouflage gear for the drill sergeant

Cast of Characters

★ Drill Sergeant U. Will Shapeup—A lead drill sergeant with a loud voice and aggressive physical presence. (If a student can't pull this off, find an adult who will play the part. Choose your drill sergeant carefully. This is the perfect opportunity to choose one of your high energy young men to lead the performance, and you might want to give him the script a week in advance so he can memorize the script. He should feel free to ad-lib a Drill Sergeant persona for full effect—saying, "I can't hear you!" and repeat questions for a louder response, and add random push-ups if necessary.)

★ Cadets 1, 2, and 3

★ All Other Cadets (all students)

Helps and Hints for Middle Schoolers

Our western culture values independence over group structure. This often leads us to resist the instructions of those in authority over us. "Marching to the beat of your own drum" is a theme that appeals to most middle schoolers. Doing what you're told or asked can result in a trumpet call for rebellion as preteens try to prove their independence. Logic doesn't work well either. However, humor can mobilize young teens better than stringent demands.

As you teach and encourage them, don't tone down what God says. Instead, give students a reason to behave in godly ways. Reward the right kind of actions and talk—as God does—and keep asking them to evaluate for themselves, "Whose instructions am I listening to, and why?"

I Don't Know, but I've Been Told

*The curtain opens with **Drill Sergeant Shapeup** standing in front of **Cadets** who are standing at attention in two- or three-line formations, depending on the number of participants.*

Drill Sergeant Shapeup: *(pacing up and down the line of **Cadets**)* Why are you here? To learn discipline! Forget about being soft and spineless. You've gotta fight for what's right and get with God's program! I'm here to show you the kind of discipline God expects from His people. And I've been told you have a lot to learn.

Let's see what you've learned so far. When I give the word, I want you to march like you've been trained in boot camp. Ready . . . MARCH! *(in cadence)* Left . . . right . . . left . . . right . . . left. . . .

*(Unpracticed **Cadets** march in disorderly fashion, some moving left, some right. They bump into each other and look awkward and sheepish.)*

Drill Sergeant Shapeup: STOP! STOP! That's the sorriest marching formation I've ever seen! Just because you're wearing the uniform and standing in line doesn't make you a soldier! *(He stands in front of one **Cadet** in the front row.)* What about you? Huh? What was that I just saw? Are you a real soldier—or are you a fake? *(**Cadet** nervously nods head in agreement, then shakes it in disagreement.)*

*(Stands in front of another **Cadet**)* And what about you? Are you ready to get in line? Or do you plan to go your own way? *(**Cadet** looks left, then right, as if hoping somebody will give him the answer. Then shrugs.)*

Okay, okay. We need to start from scratch. First lesson, military cadence. When I shout out a line, you will repeat it. You WILL march in rhythm.

*(**Drill Sergeant** shouts off the following cadence, following the familiar "Sound Off" rhythm. After each line, the **Cadets** repeat. Everyone marches in place to the rhythm.)*

I don't know but I've been told,

It takes work to make us bold.

When we do what God commands

We can finally take a stand.

If I'm sleeping during this drill

I can't do my Father's will.

Sergeant: Sound off!

Cadets: *(in unison)* 1–2

Sergeant: Sound off!

Cadets: 3–4

Sergeant: 1–2–3–4

Cadets: 1–2 . . . 3–4!

*(On the last 3–4, the **Cadets** stop marching abruptly, looking crisp and disciplined.)*

Sergeant: Now that's better! Let's see what you can remember. *(Stands in front of **Cadet 1**, talking loudly)* What does God demand of his people?

Cadet 1: Discipline, Sir!

Sergeant: Are you ready to work hard and do what's right?

Cadet 1: Yes, Sir!

Sergeant: *(to Cadet 2)* Are you going to march in line with God or do your own thing?

Cadet 2: March in line with God, Sir!

Sergeant: *(to Cadet 3)* Are you going to follow His rules or look like a fool?

Cadet 3: Follow His rules, Sir!

Sergeant: Now we're getting somewhere. There's no such thing as marching to your own drum here. The enemy is fierce and the battle is long. Only a disciplined follower of God has a chance to survive. Are we ready?

All Cadets: *(with enthusiasm)* YES, SIR!

Sergeant: Let's take it home, cadets!

*(All march off stage as the **Drill Sergeant** chants and **Cadets** echo the final cadence.)*

We will train with all our might

So that we can do what's right.

We won't stop until we're done,

Till the battle's fought and won.

God will be our one true guide;

He will always take our side.

(The sound fades out.)

Curtain Call

Prompt students to apply the lesson truth by discussing it together.

★ **This skit was obviously an exaggeration. God isn't a drill sergeant. But what elements of the skit mirror God's truth about following instructions?** *(God expects obedience. He wants us to do what's right and won't tolerate disobedience. God's way of doing things results in a better life—not obeying is the weak way to live.)*

★ **Why is obedience so critical?** *(When you obey, it shows that you respect and trust God. When you obey, you will go the direction God knows is best for you. Obedience protects you from bad consequences and from being vulnerable to Satan.)*

★ **What are some potential results of choosing not to obey God?** *(losing closeness with Him, being unprotected from Satan, God's judgment, getting caught up in worldly things that can bring you pain, destruction, and loss, etc.)*

★ **Why is obeying God and doing right so hard?** *(Because it goes against our human nature; Satan is fighting it and uses temptations to lure us away. We want to do things our way. Obeying isn't always fun or easy or the most desirable thing. It can cause us to lose friends. We don't always trust that God knows us or what's best for us.)*

Dear Jeremiah

Bible Basis:

Jeremiah 1:4-10; 20:7-11; 23:28-29

Memory Verse:

Before I formed you in the womb
I knew you, before you were born
I set you apart.
Jeremiah 1:5

Bible Background

It's easy to praise sturdy old Jeremiah—an Old Testament prophet who, despite being stretched to the limit, persevered through troubled times and came out triumphantly. Of course, God had a plan for His servant long before Jeremiah ever knew it. The same could be said of our own lives.

Few of us have as dramatic a revelation as Jeremiah did when God told him about the plan for his life. And yet God has prepared in advance good works for us to do (Eph. 2:10). Before we were capable of talking, walking, working, or acquiring possessions, we were formed by God's hand.

When God first told Jeremiah of his appointment as a prophet, Jeremiah felt hugely inadequate. Who wouldn't, especially when young, inexperienced, and facing a daunting assignment? God didn't accept Jeremiah's protests about the task; He knew the job and that Jeremiah was the right one for it. God valued Jeremiah, who would turn out to be an incredibly faithful, unswerving voice against Judah's stubbornness.

Jeremiah repeatedly expressed God's words against heavy odds. And God continued to support His mouthpiece, whose words remain today as cautions and reminders of truth in a dark land. Jeremiah was valuable to God, and we're valuable in that way also.

Along with Jeremiah, Paul, Isaiah, and Daniel are others who were chosen by God to do His work. None was worthy apart from God's investment of His Spirit and power, and neither are we. Yet because of His calling on our lives, we become valuable to God and to others beyond measure.

Summary

Hearing that they were formed in the mind of God before they were born, students are prompted to write an individual letter sent to him or her by God.

This writing assignment, which asks your students to write from God's perspective, can be tricky without the right setup. Prompt your group to find the biblical basis for God's "voice" rather than merely speculating about His character. If various Psalms tell us that God created our "inmost being" (139:13), then we can assume that God has intimate knowledge of our thoughts and motives. Remind them that it is never wise to assign motives to God that contradict the Holy Scriptures.

While the following exercise is not theatrical, you might consider having students participate in an oral reading.

Setting

None

Materials

★ Stationery or lined binder paper
★ Pens and pencils
★ Bibles

Procedure

Using the following biblical passages, spend some time sharing with your group just how valuable God views each one of them to be.

Jeremiah 1:4–10	Psalm 139	Ephesians 2:10
Luke 12:6–7	Ezekiel 34:11–12	

Have students spend time alone, writing a letter addressed to themselves, which shares through God's voice how He feels about His children—them!

Read sample letters out loud first to give them ideas, if you think it best. Leave them out for students to use to get ideas.

Helps and Hints for Middle Schoolers

Not every adolescent is comfortable writing letters. Texting and digital communication have replaced many traditional writing forms; not surprisingly, many young people have abandoned letter writing in favor of quicker, more superficial responses. Expect that some preteens are going to balk at this activity or find it very challenging. Try to just get them started, and let them continue at home if necessary. Follow up with them during the week with encouragement. You could give them a couple of suggestions of what God might say to them and see if they can take it from there. If writing a regular length letter is too uncomfortable, you could ask them to try it as an email or postcard.

Dear Jeremiah

The following samples are fictional letters written in God's "voice" to His children.

Sample Letter #1

Dear Andrew,

I'm looking down on you from heaven and I like what I see. You remind Me of a super-powered performance race car. You've got lots of good ideas, and I already put inside you everything you need to run a great race. I knew before you were born exactly who and what you would be. You're going to love it!

I have big plans for you, but you can't see them yet. I can use how you draw and design things to make something cool out of you. You don't know what it is yet, but keep waiting. You have to keep on the right track. I need you to trust Me, and I'll give you strength and courage along the way.

Look at the examples I gave you to follow. Read the Bible and try to be like Jeremiah and David. Look at grown-ups who follow Me in your church and school. They'll help you. I love you a lot!

God

Sample Letter #2

Dear Brooke,

I am God and I love you. I know you better than anyone else in the world—even better than your parents and your best friends. I understand you better than they ever will. I made you like a treasured teacup—beautiful and useful. Whether you are close to Me or far from Me, I love you just the same.

I am the one who picked out your hair color and your eye color. I made your personality and your talents. You're like a caterpillar that will become a butterfly. Even when you don't like who you are and the way you look, I know you. When you think you're not good enough, remember, I made you and I only make lovely and useful things.

Don't believe other people who tell you "you aren't good enough" or "you aren't pretty enough." I made beautiful things in you that they can't see. It's going to be all right.

You are totally secure in My hands. Even the ugly things in the world around you aren't stronger than Me. I'm God and you're Mine. Trust Me.

Love,
Your Father in Heaven

Curtain Call

Though the topic is quite personal, stimulate conversation among the group to help them find more application in the topic of their value to God.

★ **What are some signs that God values you in your life right now?** *(My family loves me. I have opportunities to serve God. I have a great youth group. My friends value me. I feel like I have a purpose in life.)*

★ **What kinds of things in the world work against the truth that you are valuable to God?** *(media images and messages, the way people treat each other badly or unfairly, being ignored or overlooked, not fitting into the "right" groups, not having athletic or other talents that some people have, being different from others makes you feel worthless, etc.)*

★ **In what ways can God use a person your age for His purposes?** *(sharing Jesus with others, helping those around me, caring for the less fortunate, being a witness to the people in my social group, praising Him and worshiping Him, being a good example to peers and younger kids, etc.)*

★ **Where can you find reinforcement to help you live in the truth that God values you?** *(being with Christian friends, at church, the Bible, Christian music, adults who believe in me, talking to God, etc.)*

**Before I formed you in the womb
I knew you,
before you were born
I set you apart.
Jeremiah 1:5**

Fraud Buster, Private Eye

Bible Basis:

Jeremiah 14:14; 22:3; 23:2, 26; 28:15

Memory Verse:

Sanctify them by the truth;
your word is truth.
John 17:17

Bible Background

Fakers have existed for centuries. Whether it was a false prophet during the long-ago days of Nebuchadnezzar or a modern television guru peddling deceptive promises, fakers know how to sell their story. Even more disturbing is that people continue to listen and believe them, including Christians who could use God's own Word to test the messages they hear, but fail to do so.

It's been this way since Israel's early days. Jeremiah, whose name means "May Yahweh lift up," and the other Old Testament prophets, were continually warning the Jews to stop being led off the right path by those who lied and deceived them. Jeremiah began his work as a voice for God in 627 B.C.; he soon recognized that people generally listened to what they wanted to hear. Listening to a smooth talker who made their sins sound reasonable and excusable was much preferred to hearing announcements of judgment that God's true prophets often delivered. In contrast, the true voices for God were mistreated, ignored, and lived frugally; suffering was often a prophet's earthly reward for sharing God's news.

To prevent false prophets from continuing to lead Israel astray, God outlined several tests of a true prophet: loyalty to Yahweh (the Lord God), accurate fulfillment of future predictions, and agreement with previous revelations.

Today we can still use these tests to spot false teachers. If we're objective and willing to know the truth, we can also see that the deceivers usually stand to gain fame or material goods from their false teaching, and that they themselves don't live according to God's standards. We should hold each Christian teacher, leader, and evangelist up to the light and let their deeds and words prove whether they are truly of God, or just fakers.

Summary

Fraud Buster and his team of private investigators must decide which $20 bills are authentic and which are fakes. The head of the squad comes up with a brilliant plan to foil the ring of counterfeiters. Using the genre of a detective show, this skit illustrates a familiar counterfeit analogy: The best way to detect a fake is to know the original inside and out.

Setting

Detective's office set up with table for desk and 2-3 chairs

Props

- ★ A desk with a desk lamp
- ★ 2-3 chairs
- ★ Folders, stacks of paperwork, a briefcase
- ★ A $20 bill in the briefcase

Cast of Characters

- ★ Narrator, with a gift for deadpan humor and a dramatic-sounding voice
- ★ Fraud Buster, lead detective

Private Investigators

- ★ Snooper
- ★ Scratchy
- ★ Sniffy

Helps and Hints for Middle Schoolers

No one wants to admit he or she has been fooled, but often learning by experience is a valuable means of gaining wisdom and discernment. Don't put middle schoolers on the spot by making them share personal experiences where they've been foolish or wrong, but if any want to describe a way they were deceived and how they figured out the truth, their experiences can be powerful for other preteens. Young people can be very vulnerable to deceitful leaders and deceptive thinking since their own critical thinking skills are still rudimentary. You can help by explaining that anyone is fair game for counterfeit beliefs, and that they can fight back by knowing what's true. These skills will begin to provide young teens a sense of self-confidence that can help them stand for truth rather than give in to whatever sounds good or is the popular stance.

Fraud Buster, Private Eye

*The scene opens with **Fraud Buster** sitting at his paper-strewn desk, perhaps in the glare of a single spotlight. He diligently leans over his work as the **Narrator** reads offstage.*

Narrator: *(in the dry style of old detective shows, with melodramatic intensity)* Fraud Buster knew that his days were numbered. He had scoured the files for weeks, searching for a clue to crack the case once and for all. His eyes, weakened by the small print on papers that overflowed his desk, had seen too much.

Fraud knew a victory in this case would bring redemption. Unless he and his team of private investigators could discover the counterfeiting ring's secret, all would be lost.

*(The three **Private Investigators** barge into **Buster's** office.)*

Sniffy: Hey, boss, have we got news for you!

Scrappy: Yeah! Wait till you hear what we've got to tell ya'. We finally have a lead! *(motioning to Snooper's briefcase)*

Buster: Whoa, whoa . . . we haven't had a lead in weeks. What makes you think you have what we're looking for?

Snooper: Here's proof. You gotta check this out. *(**Snooper** opens his briefcase; all three look inside with great suspense as he slowly lifts a large bill into the light. All freeze with wonder in their faces as the **Narrator** reads offstage again.)*

Narrator: *(offstage)* Buster and his cronies were frequently known to create drama where there was none. Today was no exception.

Scrappy: Look at that, boss!

Sniffy: Yeah, ain't it beautiful?

Buster: What am I lookin' at? It's just a $20 bill.

Snooper: No it ain't. It's a fake.

Buster: *(grabbing it to look closer)* Are you sure? This doesn't look like the last counterfeit bill we discovered.

Snooper: I know. It's a new version. See that little mark right there? That's the difference. These counterfeiters are a tough bunch. They've used at least 15 different versions to throw us off.

Sniffy: Here's the deal, boss. If we're going to find these counterfeit bills, we're going to have to train all the retailers in the city what these 15 versions look like. That's gonna take some time.

Buster: We don't have that kind of time, Sniffy. How can we train thousands of store clerks to spot a fake, when there are so many different counterfeit bills out there?

Scrappy: Maybe we should stop and think this through again.

*(The four actors each adopt a different "thinking pose"—hand on chin, fingers on temples with eyes closed, and so forth—and freeze under the spotlight while **Narrator** speaks.)*

Narrator: (*melodramatically*) Buster and his boys knew the deceivers weren't going to give up easily. The counterfeiters were on a mission to win…but faced with the powerful intellect of four truth-seekers, their schemes were destined to fail. Soon they would uncover the solution … (*long pause while four actors look as though they're ready to speak, but then return to their thoughtful poses*) soon (*pause*) …almost there now ….

Scrappy: I've got it!

Buster: I love you, man! (***Scrappy*** *and* ***Buster*** *bang fists together.*) What do ya' got?

Scrappy: Instead of training every clerk in the city what the fakes look like, let's just make them real familiar with what the original looks like—up and down, inside and out!

Snooper: Yeah! If they really know what the original looks like, they'll spot a fake easily.

Sniffy: You're brilliant, man. Brilliant!

Buster: So we gotta come up with some training to teach everyone to study the real deal. Yeah, that seems a lot better than trying to memorize all the frauds. (*pauses*) Okay, who's on it? (*puts hand out*)

Sniffy: I'm in! (*throwing hand to the middle, as in team solidarity*)

Scrappy: Me too, boss! (*adds hand to the first*)

Snooper: Count me in! (*throws hand on top, and all four freeze one last time*)

Buster: (*turns to student audience*) How about the rest of you novice crime stoppers? Are you with us? (*The three PIs run out into the crowd, high-fiving and slapping students on the arm like comrades.*)

Narrator: (*offstage*) In the dim haze of a late summer afternoon, just when crime was ready to rule the streets, Fraud Buster and his private eyes took back the city once and for all.

Curtain Call

Continue to develop students' understanding of the topic by interacting.

★ **How is the Bible like a real $20 bill?** (*It's worth something. It has real value. It can be trusted and used the way it was intended. You can have confidence in it. You know you won't be taken for a ride when you use it.*)

★ **Do you need to know all the false religions and world philosophies to be able to tell what's real and what isn't?** (*No, if you know the genuine Scripture and what God has said, you can judge every other philosophy and religion against the Bible and tell what is true. The Bible is like a ruler you can use to check out any other way of thinking or believing; if those other ways don't measure up to the Bible, they aren't true.*)

★ **How can you be smart and protect yourself from being deceived by false truth and wrong thinking?** (*Know the Bible; keep reading and studying it to really understand what God has said; listen to those who speak and teach the truth; be willing to admit you're wrong when you've started to trust in what is false; ask God to show you what's true and what isn't.*)

Danny Dawg and the Master G

Bible Basis:

Daniel 1:8-17

Memory Verse:

The fear of the LORD teaches a man wisdom, and humility comes before honor.
Proverbs 15:33

Bible Background

Who doesn't find something to love about Daniel? A young Israelite with courage and conviction, of royal heritage, Daniel ended up in Babylon as a captive. Daniel and three other young Jewish men were among those required to complete a course of study that would one day position them as future advisors to King Nebuchadnezzar.

Nebuchadnezzar was the ruler of the world's most powerful nation at that time in history. He conquered other countries and usually took back to Babylon the most valuable citizens to augment his population. Part of Nebuchadnezzar's plan to assimilate foreigners into his country involved changing their names. In the case of the Jewish captives, the king also required that they eat his prescribed foods—items that were forbidden to Jews who kept God's law. Of course, this king and future kings whom Daniel would serve demanded religious allegiance from the foreigners.

Daniel and his contemporaries who refused to honor any God but Yahweh used their wits. They acquired plenty of knowledge about Babylon and its ways but didn't let their head knowledge affect their heart devotion. Daniel survived and even prospered in Babylon because he worked his hardest, served the king loyally, maintained his integrity, and refused to be distracted from the true God. During his 60 years in Babylon, he served Belshazzar, Darius, and Cyrus in addition to Nebuchadnezzar.

Summary

Select several students to memorize and perform different portions of a modern rap describing the experiences of Daniel and his friends in the king's court.

While rap as an art form can evoke negative connotations, it can also be a clever and interesting way of using rhythm and word play to tell stories. Raps are not to be recited like standard poetry; in fact, they sound awkward without some improvisational rhythm.

Allow your students to practice different interpretations of these lines. In addition you could encourage them to use pantomime as they recite. Choose several performers, giving each a section to memorize and perform for the group.

Setting

Empty stage as background for modern rap

Props

★ No props are required, but some students might want to add small props (food items, free weights, a crown, etc.) to add interest and humor to various aspects of the script.

Cast of Characters

★ Several confident students to be rappers (sometimes called MCs).

Helps and Hints for Middle Schoolers

No one wants to have to take a stand, especially if you feel like you are standing alone. Middle school kids are particularly sensitive to feeling isolated. Today's culture can leave kids feeling like they always have to fit in—with their clothing, music, even their lifestyles and moral standards. Encourage your students that God will give them strength to resist the temptations they face and creative solutions like Daniel, even if they have to stand alone.

Danny Dawg and the Master G

We're here to tell a tale with a happy ending.

It's bound to bring a smile with the message I'm sending.

But before the finale, we gotta tell you the beginning.

It'll have you grinnin', but remember the tale I'm spinnin'

Is all about a guy like you who's tempted to go on sinnin'.

Let me share my collection of tight tongue twisters;

It's especially right for all you brothers and sisters

Who get close to the fire, but don't wanna get blisters.

See, a young man named Daniel—he had every opportunity.

He was strong and noble, and the king gave him immunity.

This Daniel, he was the man with all the royal training,

Given all the best, but wanting to be restraining.

Given good steaks and wine—forget the vegetarian;

The royal family hoped they could bribe and even bury him

In all the fancy goods that a palace could offer him.

They even changed his name and hoped his old friends would scoff at him.

But Daniel was pretty unhappy about this royal diet.

He knew that it might turn him soft if he should go and try it.

It could only lead to trouble—make him lose his edge, get fatter.

The palace staff was worried and asked what was the matter?

But when Daniel asked for healthy food, it only made them sadder,

And they were afraid, instead of fruit, their heads would be on the platter.

But Daniel asked a steward that he felt could be trusted,

And this guy took a chance even though he might be busted.

Daniel and his friends requested water and asparagus

And said "After ten short days, you will be comparin' us

To all the other fellas who were eatin' steak and darin' us.

You can look us up and down and notice that we are strong

And then you make your choice and see if we were wrong."

Ten days of the experiment proved the winner would be God;

Instead of *drinking* six packs, Danny got one on his bod.

Danny and his posse had discovered how to win,

And it wasn't by acting tough and choosing pleasure on a whim,

But by following the Lord's command instead of chasing sin.

The story doesn't end right there—it's got a tight conclusion.

Daniel and his pack of friends were more than an illusion.

Breaking through the confusion, their competitors were losin'.

And when it came to Daniel, the king knew he had to choose him,

Danny was the man, but it wasn't just some magic;

If you don't obey the rules, the results just might be tragic.

Curtain Call

Stimulate discussion and constructive debate among students as they assimilate the truth of this lesson.

★ **What changes was Daniel willing to make to please his new king?** *(He accepted his new name, was willing to serve the king, had a positive attitude about his new home and position, was respectful, tried to learn what he was taught, and worked to get along with the other authorities such as the palace master.)*

★ **In what areas was Daniel unwilling to bend?** *(anything that required him to go against God's law or God's ways, to eat the king's food and drink the wine which was forbidden for Israelites, etc.)*

★ **How did Daniel creatively work it out so he could please the king while not going against his faith?** *(He came up with a plan. He devised a test that would show the palace master and king that his ways of following God were better than theirs. He wasn't defiant or stubborn. He tried to prevent anyone from being embarrassed or punished for his choices.)*

★ **How can Daniel's example help you work creatively with those in authority over you?** *(Students will have a variety of ideas; affirm all that are responsible and workable.)*

Casino Babylon

Bible Basis:

Daniel 5:1–18, 20, 21d–31

Memory Verse:

If my people, who are called by my name, will humble themselves and pray and seek my face and turn from their wicked ways, then will I hear from heaven and will forgive their sin and will heal their land.

2 Chronicles 7:14

Bible Background

Some leaders achieve legendary stature, but Belshazzar's fame was far from noble. As the king of Babylonia, Belshazzar ruled a huge empire in the Middle East. He built fancy, terraced temples, employed 100 noblemen, and flaunted his wealth at enormous indulgent parties.

But Belshazzar let all his pomp and power go to his head, and he ended up gloating about his own greatness and forgetting about God's majesty. Belshazzar's arrogance spurred him to use the sacred vessels stolen from the Jewish temple in Jerusalem for his party guests' drinks; even more appalling, he praised the gods of the gold, iron, and stone that the vessels were made from. It wasn't long before his gambling days were over.

God had enough of Belshazzar's audacious disrespect so He sent the king a startling message— written by a disembodied hand on a wall where Belshazzar was holding his bash. Finally, the king was shocked to a standstill and became desperate to find someone who could interpret the three Aramaic words on the wall. Daniel, now approximately 80 years old, was the only one who had the interpretation—and it wasn't pretty. God's message charged Belshazzar with three sins: disobedience, desecration of sacred objects, and idolatry. God made it clear that this blatant disregard for His truth wouldn't be tolerated, and that night Belshazzar died. Belshazzar's consequence was an unforgettable example to all those present that God would not be mocked or belittled.

Summary

While using other people's money, a group of gamblers plays a solemn game of life and death. In the tradition of classic morality plays, young actors portray the danger that comes from flaunting sin and false power. When the roulette wheel finally comes up on the wrong color, everyone will have to pay.

Setting

A gambling establishment

Props

★ Several decks of cards
★ A pair of dice
★ A roulette wheel (real or drawn)
★ Miscellaneous "casino" tables
★ Coins and cash (real or fake)

Cast of Characters

★ Bonehead Bubba
★ High Stakes Henry
★ Duke the Dissuader (the voice of reason)
★ Gracie Gambler
★ Casino Dealers 1, 2, and 3
★ Offstage Narrator

Helps and Hints for Middle Schoolers

It's hard for young people, who are naturally self-centered, to consider world affairs or national issues. However, this particular lesson brings down to their level the broader consequences of nations who embrace wickedness and categorically reject God. Young people often rationalize behavior by blaming their bad choices on others or circumstances. Point out their faulty reasoning if they hold up bad leadership or cultural traditions as reasons why it's okay to go against God's guidelines. Motivate them to take the initiative to stand unswervingly on their God-based beliefs and go against the culture as a method of inspiring change. Encourage youth to support each other (invoke that peer power) in their faith so they stand together instead of falling.

Casino Babylon

*As the scene opens, three **Casino Dealers** are shuffling cards and tossing dice at their respective tables. The **Narrator** speaks from offstage.*

Narrator: The year is 600 B.C. and Casino Babylon is in full swing. Its gamblers are greedy and vulnerable. Bonehead Bubba has been visiting the casino for several weeks, feeling lucky and invincible. He and his friends, High Stakes Henry and Gracie Gambler, are back for another wild night. Another friend, Duke the Dissuader, stands alone, warning them to reconsider their gambling.

(The four main characters enter talking among themselves.)

Gracie Gambler: *(jingling coins in her pocket)* Can you believe that slot machine? I knew it was my lucky day.

High Stakes Henry: Aw, gee. . .I was next up on that machine. If you hadn't taken one more turn, all that money would've been mine.

Bonehead Bubba: *(Sarcastic)* Yeah, right. When has it ever been your lucky day? Gracie's been like magic all night long. I want to stay close to her. Do you realize that for the past four weeks, Gracie hasn't lost a dime?

Gracie Gambler: Hey! Look over there. *(points to a blackjack table)* I'm going to play a little blackjack. Wish me luck! *(joins the dealer and pretends to play)*

Duke the Dissuader: Listen, you guys. This is all wrong. Remember that sign out front? "GAMBLING IS STRICTLY FORBIDDEN. ENTER AT YOUR OWN RISK." Take that warning to heart, and let's get out of here.

High Stakes Henry: C'mon, Duke. You're so gutless. Someone probably put that sign there to mess with our heads. They want all the money themselves, so they're trying to keep us out.

Duke the Dissuader: Trust me, guys. I know the sign isn't just for looks. I believe what it says. I don't want you to lose your shirts. Listen, let's just go. *(**Gracie** whoops and is celebrating at the blackjack table.)*

Bonehead Bubba: Can't you hear Gracie celebrating? That sign is a joke. We can do anything we want! Look at this cash! *(pulls a fistful of cash out of his pocket)*

*(**Henry** and **Bubba** join **Gracie**; the three move from table to table collecting more winnings. **Duke** stays at a distance, shaking his head.)*

Casino Dealer 1: Attention! The roulette wheel is open! Place all your money on red or black—the choice is yours!

(The gambling trio moves to the roulette wheel, placing all their money on the table.)

Bonehead Bubbba: We're all in! No one can beat us now. We're hot! Let's put everything on red. Let 'er spin!

*(The crowd watches the wheel as it spins. As it slows down, the **Narrator** speaks.)*

Narrator: *(ominously)* Bubba! Bubba! Your time is up . . . Your decisions have been placed on the scale and found wanting. You have defied all warnings and trusted in your own power.

Duke the Dissuader: *(calling out from the side)* Oh, no. I could see this coming. If only you had listened. Now you're going to lose more than your shirt!

Bonehead Bubba: Wait! Wait! This can't happen! I can't lose all my money now!

Narrator: Oh, it's not your *money* you must give up. . . your cash won't save you now.

(The lights begin to dim.)

Gracie Gambler: *(frightened)* Here! Take the money—I don't need it anyway. *(thrusts it at the Dealer, tries to run out)*

High Stakes Henry: *(also tosses his cash at the dealer)* She's right—take it all. Just leave me alone!

Narrator: It's too late. You played when you should have walked. Now it's time to pay up.

*(Bubba moans and shakes, his knees knocking. The **Casino Dealers** grab each character and remove them from the stage while each struggles to save himself.)*

Duke the Dissuader: I wish they had listened. I tried to tell them that the writing was on the wall. They could have escaped this horrible fate. Now everything they thought they had will be someone else's gain, and they're history. What a waste! *(Walks off shaking his head sadly.)*

Curtain Call

Link personal sin to the greater reality of nations wallowing in sin through a conversation based on the skit and Scripture.

★ **Think about ancient Babylon and Belshazzar's behavior. Do you see anything similar happening in our country today?** *(addictions to gambling, sex, celebrity worship, materialism, focus on money and material things, people consumed with pleasure and self-indulgence, etc.)*

★ **How is our own nation guilty of pleasure seeking and pampering the self?** *(spending money on leisure, huge debts, buying bigger and fancier homes, cars, and luxury items, obesity because of rich but unhealthy foods, people ignoring others' needs because they're too caught up in themselves, etc.)*

★ **Belshazzar wanted immediate pleasures and immediate gratification. Is there any of that in our culture?** *(People don't want to wait to save money to buy, so they go into debt. People don't wait for marriage before becoming sexually active. There is a lack of self-discipline in taking care of their health or bodies.)*

★ **If Daniel were to speak to us today, what do you think he might tell us?** *(Stop pampering yourself and thinking so highly of yourself. Stop and think about God's ways and change your ways. Put God first instead of yourself. Be careful not to dishonor what God values.)*

A Tale of Five Piggies

Bible Basis:

Hosea 14:1-7

Memory Verse:

Create in me a pure heart, O God, and
renew a steadfast spirit within me.
Psalm 51:10

Bible Background

Hosea, a prophet who began his ministry shortly after Amos, has sometimes been called the "St. John of the Old Testament." His profound message of love and forgiveness is unlike any other. Hosea didn't just tell the Israelites that they should give up their sinfulness and return to God: He demonstrated it to them by living a real-life lesson. God instructed Hosea to marry a prostitute and show her unconditional love and acceptance, the same way God loved and wanted to forgive His people who were continually unfaithful to Him.

Israel faced some ruthless enemies, and in the process of seeking refuge, the nation adopted the pagan ways of its neighbors. God asked the Jews to admit their errors by abandoning their idolatry and coming back to Him with a sincere confession of their wrongs. They had to realize they could not save themselves, but God would readily heal them if only they would humbly repent.

Hosea's writings made it clear to the Israelites that although they would have to accept the consequences of their waywardness from God, He still deeply desired for them to return to Him so He could fully forgive them and give them a fresh start. Just like them, when we've chosen to walk away from God, we need to admit that we can't fix our sins ourselves or redeem ourselves. We can appeal to God for mercy and forgiveness and know for certain that if our hearts are sincere, God will be merciful and forgiving.

Hosea's steps to reconciliation are clear: Confess your sin, turn from your sin, and embrace God's forgiveness.

Summary

This short tale—designed to be performed for a younger group—will teach both performers and audiences alike that God's forgiveness can make us clean. Pig characters trudge through dirt, only to find out that they're not happy wallowing in the mud.

Since this play is designed for a younger audience, arrange in advance to perform for another class. It might be helpful to emphasize the importance of being a good role model before, during, and after the performance.

Setting

Farm mud puddle

Props

★ If full-scale pig costumes aren't available, use simple ears, snouts, and tails made from pink construction paper.
★ Several large, brown blankets
★ Brown paint or makeup for creating dirt streaks on the pig characters' faces

Cast of Characters

★ Narrator
★ Oinker, a pig
★ Squeaky, Oinker's best friend
Three younger pigs
★ Bristle, a pig
★ Bonnie, with bows on her ears
★ Boo, carries a blanket

Helps and Hints for Middle Schoolers

All of your students will know what it feels like to have done wrong—to be dirty as the pigs were. However, some may not have experienced forgiveness from family members or friends, so the concept of being freed from the grubbiness of their wrongs may be unfamiliar. Try to spark a conversation about what a fresh start feels like, and how to get a fresh start. You might want to role-play a couple of situations between a parent and child or two friends, with one sincerely asking forgiveness for a wrong and the other graciously giving it. It's also effective to use an object lesson: Show a beat-up backpack or piece of sports equipment, and replace it with a new one. That's what it's like when God forgives someone who is truly sorry.

A Tale of Five Piggies

Narrator: Once upon a time there were five little pigs: Squeaky, Oinker, Bristle, Bonnie, and Boo. Squeaky loved mud, but Oinker had his doubts about it.

Squeaky: Oinker! Guess what? The rain made everything gooey and mushy in the meadow. We haven't been able to get this dirty since Hammy smuggled us into the compost pile last spring. Let's go!

Oinker: Are you sure getting grimy is such a good thing? My mom said to stay clean today.

Squeaky: Listen . . . dirt is where it's at. *(Turns to audience)* Who thinks Oinker should get muddy? *(Listens to audience response.)*

Oinker: And who thinks I should do what Mom said? *(Waits for audience response.)*

(Both shrug, undecided.)

Narrator: Along came Bonnie, Bristle, and Boo.

Bristle: Hey, guys! We're just coming out to play. Wanna root around for food with us?

Bonnie: *(in a little girl voice)* We're so hungry! Come and root!

Boo: It's more fun with more pigs!

Squeaky: Uh . . . uh, well, I guess we can root for a little while. *(pauses while thinking)* But I've got a better idea. What about playing somewhere new, a place pigs can only dream about . . . ?

Oinker: *(rolling eyes, nudging **Squeaky** while whispering to him)* Squeaky, I told you we shouldn't be going there!

Squeaky: Don't listen to Oinker. He's just afraid you might have too much fun. I've found the greatest patch of mud in the south meadow. We could go there right now, roll around all day, and have the time of our lives. What do you think?

Oinker: I . . . I don't know. Mud is so sticky. It really messes me up.

Squeaky: You'll be fine. It's just mud. So who's with me?

Bristle: I think it's an awesome idea. I'll go!

Bonnie and Boo: Let's go! Let's do it! *(**Squeaky** leads the three younger pigs offstage while **Oinker** follows reluctantly, shaking his head. Lights down.)*

Narrator: The four little pigs followed Squeaky into the meadow.

*(Lights up. **Pigs** are rolling around in the brown blankets. Their faces show "mud" streaks. They ooh and aahh, making funny noises as they wallow.)*

Oinker: Wow, Squeaky. This is heaven.

Bristle: You better believe it.

Bonnie: This is the most fun I've had in months.

Boo: Look what I can do! *(Boo makes a "snow angel" motion with arms and legs in the blankets.)*

(After a brief pause, all five give a heavy sigh together.)

Squeaky: Do you guys feel kind of funny? The mud behind my ears is getting really itchy *(scratches ears)*.

Bristle: There's mud in my eyes! Ow! I can't see!

Oinker: *(speaking like he feels nauseated)* I think I'm going to be sick. I thought it would be fun to get dirty, but now I feel yucky. I need a shower!

*(**Squeaky** jumps up and down, trying to scratch himself all over. The younger pigs shake themselves, poke fingers in ears, push imaginary mud off their skin, etc. **Boo** is boo-hooing.)*

Squeaky: A shower sounds so good right now. Mud isn't all it's cracked up to be.

(All waddle uncomfortably across the stage.)

Oinker: *(arm around **Squeaky**)* We should have learned this last time we took a mud bath. Remember? It felt cool at first but then we couldn't wait to wash off. I guess it's true what they say: You can't play in the mud without it sticking to you. *(As they walk close together, the mud has literally made them stick to each other.)*

Squeaky: Last one to the river's a rotten egg. *(Others nod and grunt in agreement as they struggle to break away from each other and run offstage.)*

Narrator: So the five little piggies went to the river and washed until they were squeaky clean. Then each little piggy went wee-wee-wee all the way home. And that's the end of this pig tale. *(Actors offstage groan loudly at this painful pun.)*

Curtain Call

Draw your students into the discussion to get their thoughts after concluding the skit.

★ **How do you go about getting clean in your spirit and heart when you know you've messed up?** *(tell God how I feel and what I did, be willing to take responsibility for what I did, admit my mistake to God and, if necessary, to someone I wronged, accept God's forgiveness and let it go, etc.)*

★ **Are there things you could do that God could not forgive?** *(No, except for rejecting Jesus, there is nothing I could do that is so wrong God couldn't forgive it.)*

★ **What keeps us from pursuing forgiveness from God and from others?** *(fear of what they will do, embarrassment about what I did, shame, not sure what will happen if I admit it and ask to be forgiven, pride, etc.)*

★ **Why does God willingly forgive us when we've goofed up?** *(God loves us too much to leave us in our sin and cut off from Him. If we're sincere in our desire to be forgiven, He promises to forgive because in His Word. He wants to reconnect with us and have a closeness with us, but sin will keep us apart from Him.)*

Let's Put It on the Calendar

Bible Basis:

Zechariah 6:12-13; 9:9; 11:12-13; 12:10; 14:3-4

Memory Verse:

Everything must be fulfilled that is written about me in the Law of Moses, the Prophets and the Psalms.
Luke 24:44b

Bible Background

One of the most compelling arguments for the authenticity of Scripture is the way in which the Old Testament prophecies have been fulfilled throughout history. Zechariah, the final installment in the collection of Old Testament minor prophets, extended encouragement and hope to the Jews, but also warned that there would be difficult times and conflicts before the Messiah would come.

Zechariah lived and prophesied after the Jews had returned from exile in Babylon. They had started to rebuild God's temple in Jerusalem, but after 15 years the work got bogged down and wasn't being finished. Zechariah continued the encouragement Haggai had given to complete the temple, and then Zechariah related many prophecies about the Messiah's coming. He connected Jesus' appearance on earth with the rebuilding of the temple—though at the time he and his listeners had no idea there would be a stretch of 500 years before these prophecies were realized!

Along with Jeremiah, Zechariah said that "the Branch" would come from David's lineage to save his people. This branch would be both a priest and a king—something impossible in Judah at the time of its writing. The New Testament identifies this priest and king as Jesus (see Hebrews 4:14; 7:13-17; 8:1-2; and Revelation 19:16).

Other prophecies foretold Jesus' arrival on a donkey, the amount Judas was paid for his betrayal, the deliverance of Israel, and so forth. The fulfillment of prophecy, while complex and extensive, is an important part of biblical scholarship. This particular lesson explains some of the mystery in an age-appropriate way.

Summary

In a radio panel interview format, students hear about some mysteries of Old Testament prophecy.

Setting

Radio station studio

Props

* ★ A long table
* ★ A large table-standing microphone; make one from a cardboard tube and construction paper if necessary
* ★ An "On the Air" sign to hang behind the radio desk
* ★ Biblical costumes for the three ancient characters
* ★ A suit and tie for the modern interviewer

Cast of Characters

* ★ Calvin Curious, radio interviewer with a news anchor voice
* ★ Dr. Zach, the prophet Zechariah
* ★ Mr. Matthew, Matthew from the New Testament
* ★ John, the apostle John
* ★ Radio Station Director

Helps and Hints for Middle Schoolers

Old Testament prophecy isn't the easiest thing to teach middle school students. Such scholarship can seem out of touch with modern life, and at times can even feel mystical and confusing. Your students, however, have an expanding ability to think abstractly and organize a variety of facts and information. They may seem argumentative about biblical truth, mainly because they're increasingly able to analyze data and express themselves.

Don't let their attitudes put you off, and avoid getting into arguments. Present truth and let the Holy Spirit work on the preteens. Challenge them to examine the Bible themselves and pursue the truth, and affirm their desire to sift out fact from falsehood. Be ready to direct them to sources for greater examination, and be confident in God's ability to hone students' thinking.

Let's Put It on the Calendar

The panel of interviewers is sitting behind the table. **Calvin Curious** *is preparing his notes while the three panelists clear their throats, etc., while waiting. The* **Radio Station Director** *comes to the desk and counts down.*

Radio Station Director: Is everyone ready? Okay, 3 . . . 2 . . . 1 . . . and *(points to* **Calvin***)* We're on the air!

Calvin Curious: Thank you for tuning in today's radio broadcast. I'm Calvin Curious, with me today are three guests who will attempt to answer the question, "Is the Old Testament just another fairy tale?" Our first panelist is Dr. Zechariah, coming to us all the way from 520 B.C.

Dr. Zach: Greetings, Calvin. Thank you for inviting me.

Calvin: Also, we're pleased to have Matthew, my New Testament buddy who hails from the city of Galilee. How are you doing today, Matt?

Matt: I'm great, Calvin. So happy to join you for this discussion.

Calvin: And finally, the apostle John. Welcome!

John: Thank you very much, sir.

Calvin: Well, let's dive right into the discussion. Many people in our listening audience might not know that the Old Testament and the New Testament have a lot in common.

John: That's right. Many things the prophets predicted so long ago have already come true—especially the prophecies about the Messiah, our risen Lord Jesus Christ.

Calvin: That's a rather bold statement. Want to expand on that thought?

John: Certainly. I was a witness the day that Jesus rode into Jerusalem on a donkey's colt. That was just before His crucifixion. Dr. Zach's book revealed that very thing would happen.

Dr. Zach: That's right, John. I couldn't figure out at the time why God had Jesus riding on a donkey's colt. After all, Jesus was royalty! But now I see it. Jesus wasn't some hot shot like other rulers of His time. He was making a statement about peace and humility—not military strength or worldly power.

Matt: I have another example. I recorded in my book the facts surrounding a guy who earned a sweet price—30 pieces of silver, to be exact—for turning Jesus over to the authorities. But he ended up paying an even higher price.

Calvin: Interesting! And that brings us to today's call-in contest. Let's open up the phone lines for our listeners to respond to this question. Who was the guy who Dr. Zechariah predicted would receive 30 shekels for his betrayal? Call now!

(Lights dim on the panel as the **Radio Station Director** *encourages students in audience to raise their hands if they know the answer. He chooses one, asks that student's name. Lights back up on the panel.)*

Radio Station Director: Calvin, we have (student's name) on the line.

Calvin: Welcome, (name). Do you know who received 30 silver shekels for betraying Jesus? *(Judas)* You're right! Congratulations. You win a gift pack of Locusts and Honey All Natural Promised Land Snacks. Now let's return to our panel of Old and New Testament authorities. I heard somewhere that you guys collaborated on some other news . . . without even realizing you were doing it. Give us the scoop on that.

Dr. Zach: Well, I actually called Jesus "the Branch" thousands of years ago. God told me this branch would rebuild the temple. Sounded pretty strange. Much later, New Testament writers like Paul explained that Christians are God's temple. Jesus didn't build an actual temple. He created a vast kingdom made up of people from all over the world.

Calvin: Now guys, what do you say to your critics and scoffers? I mean, come on. Couldn't this all just be a series of coincidences? Stranger things have happened. . . .

Dr. Zach: I'm a pretty smart guy, Cal, but I'm no magician! There are just too many details that all came out precisely as predicted. No, they couldn't possibly be coincidences. Only God could have come up with this intricate puzzle.

Matt: I agree. Hey, I just wrote down what happened. I'm not the sharpest nail in the toolbox, but I know what I saw, and I saw things come true that Dr. Zach had predicted.

John: Same here. I read Dr. Zach's book, and I witnessed his prophecies coming true too.

Calvin: Hmm. There's obviously much more to debate, er, discuss about this intriguing connection between past and present. Do you guys have a book our listeners can order?

Dr. Zach: Definitely. It's still on the bestseller list, in fact. It's called the Bible.

Calvin: Well, we're out of time. Thanks to the sponsors of today's broadcast, Locusts and Honey Health Foods and the Prophetic Wearhouse. I hope you've gleaned some useful facts from these panelists. Thank you for tuning in. Join us next time when we look into where many Old Testament books got their weird names.

Curtain Call

Bring the prophecy lesson truth down to personal application with this discussion.

★ **What about Zechariah's predictions is most confusing or difficult for you to understand?** *(Students will have varied responses. Accept reasonable responses by affirming students' thinking.)*

★ **Does it matter that many predictions about Jesus were actually made 500 years before He came, and that He fulfilled them?** *(It means the Bible is true, that we can believe and trust what God says, that Jesus is who He said He is.)*

★ **How can you use this knowledge?** *(to help others see who Jesus is, to show skeptics that the Bible is true, to bolster my own faith when doubts come, etc.)*

★ **Does knowing about Old Testament prophecies that have been fulfilled help you to understand prophecies that are still not fulfilled? Why?** *(We can trust and believe that they will be fulfilled because God has brought so many other ones to reality already. It gives hope and deeper faith in the Bible and helps us know more about what will happen in the future.)*

Hope in the Hallway

Bible Basis:

Malachi 1:1, 5, 11; 2:8; 3:1-4

Memory Verse:

O LORD God Almighty, who is like you?
You are mighty, O LORD, and your
faithfulness surrounds you.
Psalm 89:8.

Bible Background

When a prophet comes to town, get ready for some drama. Malachi's name means "my messenger," and like many of the prophets, he spoke of warnings and promises, curses and blessings.

Malachi's message to the Israelites was a familiar one as he rebuked them for their unfaithfulness. They married unbelievers, worshiped idols, dabbled in sorcery, and showed little mercy to orphans and widows in the community. Malachi let the sparks fly. The priests themselves were not faithful to God, so it wasn't any surprise that the people were so far off the mark also.

Malachi's desire was to get the Israelites back on track to walk with their God and to receive the blessings He wanted to shower on them. After his strong scolding, Malachi added the up side—God was and continues to be eager to forgive and restore hope. Malachi wanted to impress on the Jews that God wanted a relationship with them, the one thing He had been desiring ever since He called the Israelites His own.

The closing chapters of Malachi contain clear and comforting promises concerning the hope of a Messiah. This book is a link between the Old Testament and the New, and promises that God's mercy can provide light in the darkness despite the Israelites'—and our own—unfaithfulness.

Summary

Just like the children of Israel, who were unfaithful time and time again, three students wait outside the principal's office to face consequences for their misdoings. By the end of this short play, each character discovers hope through the promises of God.

Setting

The hall of a school outside the principal's office.

Cast of Characters

★ Derek, student/wrongdoer
★ Jason, student/wrongdoer
★ Brady, student/wrongdoer
★ Narrator: randomly choose an audience member for this one-liner
★ Emcee: teacher or youth sponsor

Props

★ Bench or 3 chairs
★ Fake door (drawn on butcher paper) with 'Mr. Bates, Principal' sign on it

Helps and Hints for Middle Schoolers

Young teens, despite their silly grins and goofy jokes, can feel the despair of hopelessness. They can be prone to depression resulting from family dysfunction, friendships failing, bullying, body image issues, or as a result of drug or alcohol abuse.

Often a preteen's view of a situation is out of proportion, or the consequences can obscure the possibilities of a more positive future. Bring out God's mercy and forgiveness that are freely available when we recognize our wrongs and decide to change. And for situations a preteen can't remedy by a behavior reversal, offer support and truth about God's compassion and His ability to carry us through even the darkest times.

Hope in the Hallway

Derek, Jason, and Brady are waiting outside the principal's office to be disciplined for their wrongdoings at school.

Derek: This is getting old.

Jason: No kidding. I wait around outside Mr. B's office more than I hang out at the mall.

Derek: *(sarcastically)* You mean your parents let you out of the house? I've been on restriction since summer. Dude, if you've been to the mall since then, you're living high.

Brady: Oh yeah? It's bad enough sitting here waiting to meet my doom. I don't want to think about what my dad will do when he finds out I'm suspended again.

Derek: I dunno, Brady. At least this gets us outta that stupid math class. I hate all that stuff. Who needs to know about rational numbers and compounding interest?

Jason: I don't like it either. But I have to pass it, or I can't be on the baseball team. And this isn't gonna help at all. How did I end up here anyway? *(slouches further in his seat)*

Brady: We can't blame anybody but ourselves. We knew the rules. Mr. B made it clear last time: Don't vandalize school property, no food fights, watch our language, and don't diss the teachers. How did we end up in this hopeless hallway?

Narrator in audience: Derek Robertson, come into my office.

Derek: *(slowly stands, drooping like he's been beaten)* Yep, hopeless. Well, here goes. *(walks into the "office")*

Jason: *(stands and kicks at the chair while complaining)* I was making C's up until now. If I get suspended, I'm gonna be cut from the team. And my dad will make me quit my job at the store. I knew what I needed to do to get through this year, and what did I do? I blew it royally.

Brady: We're all in the same boat. Get real; we're total failures. Derek's right. It's hopeless.

(The two fidget, mutter to themselves, and generally look hopeless for 10-20 seconds. Dim lights. Have an Emcee ask audience members for their input about what they think will happen next. After responses have has been shared, bring lights up and continue. Mr. B's door opens and Derek comes out. He pauses by the guys.)

Jason: So, how long is your suspension?

Derek: Zero. I'm going back to class.

Brady: Huh?

Derek: You will never guess what happened in there. Mr. B wants to see you next, Jason.

Jason: *(apprehensive)* What kind of punishment did you get? Did he call your parents?

Derek: Yep. And yours, too. *(Jason and Brady mutter, slouch)* But . . . *(long pause)* he has a plan for you.

Jason: Right. We get front row seats in the detention room.

Derek: Yeah, and we deserve it. You won't believe it, but Mr. B wants to give us a new start. He gave me the chance to apologize . . . and he forgave me. I can't understand it, but he said he wants to give us some hope for our future.

Brady: *(surprised)* You're joking.

Derek: No way! It doesn't make sense to me either. But he's convinced we can change. He even said he wants to show compassion to us. Can you believe it? *(laughs)* He's setting up some kind of work and study deal so we can keep going to class while we make up for what we did.

(The three friends look disbelievingly at each other, trying to make sense of this unexpected turn of events.)

Brady: Well, yeah. Apologizing sounds good. I never thought Mr. B would want to forgive us for acting so out of control.

Jason: *(does a hand-slapping action with Derek)* Wahoo! Things look totally different now. My dad'll be mad, but maybe he'll forgive me, too.

Brady: Hey, maybe this is just a scam. Maybe Mr. B wants to really come down on us hard and is just trying to make it more ugly.

Derek: You don't get it. He's not coming down on us, he's giving us a clean start. Just take it, man. Go in and get it over with. You've got a hope of getting past this.

*(The three friends smile at each other and give each other high fives as **Jason** enters the office. **Derek** walks offstage. Lights dim.)*

Curtain Call

Make the truth of the Scripture and the skit more real and personal with this discussion.

★ **Why did the three friends end up outside the principal's office?** *(They had broken the rules again, made bad choices.)*

★ **Do you think they deserved the possible consequences of suspension, restriction, angry parents, loss of athletic opportunities, and lost jobs?** *(Yes, they knowingly did what was wrong and knew they could be caught and punished. They deserved what was coming to them. Some students may disagree.)*

★ **Why do you think the principal seemed willing to forgive the students and give them a chance to change, instead of giving them the punishment they knew they deserved?** *(He wanted to give them a chance to change for the better. He was merciful and compassionate. He thought they needed something positive to look forward to. He believed they could change if he helped them start over.)*

★ **What gave these three hope instead of discouragement and depression?** *(the belief that they could be forgiven, that someone believed in them enough to help them try again, that they wouldn't have only pain and doom to look forward to, etc.)*

★ **How does this story relate to our relationship with God?** *(Even after we mess up and have fallen away from walking with God, we can come back and start over and God will give us another chance. God wants to lift us up from our troubles and give us hope that the future isn't a dead end. We can go to God and confess what we've done and know He will give us another chance. There's always hope with God.)*

Where's Your Pride?

Bible Basis:

Matthew 7:7-11; Hebrews 12:5b-10;
Proverbs 18:24

Memory Verse:

A new command I give you:
Love one another. As I have loved you,
so you must love one another.
John 13:34

Bible Background

Parents: maddening, protective, embarrassing . . . and God-ordained. Yes, God puts families together in fascinating ways, and sometimes we just can't figure out why ours looks like it does. But God has a way of using even crazy families as object lessons to teach us His ways.

In chapter seven of the Sermon on the Mount, Jesus gives us principles of living in both spiritual and earthly families. He uses the example of a parent and a child, knowing that we will understand that parents desire good things for their children. In an even stronger way, God wants and gives the best to us—even if we can't see it or grasp it at the time.

In Hebrews, God illustrates the value of discipline. As the perfect parent, God will discipline those He loves in order to build character and wisdom. Young people generally understand that their parents' discipline isn't about punishment just for cruelty's sake—it's about training and instilling in them the traits and control needed to handle life on their own. As kids mature they are able to respect their parents' discipline instead of reacting negatively to it, and that's what God desires us to do as His children when He sets us straight after we've gone off track.

Proverbs succinctly pinpoints the loyalty a true friend—and one's family—exhibits; again a comparison demonstrates the principle best.

Besides being a cocoon where youngsters can grow safely and well, the family is a model for God's bigger community, His family of believers, where we learn about God Himself and His ways.

Summary

A pride of dysfunctional lions realizes that God uses the family structure to teach them character, wisdom, and discipline. As an allegory of sorts, this skit doesn't require lion costumes to be effective; the language itself will guide the audience to understand the characters. However, if the actors would like to add simple props—tails, whiskers, ears, or landscape features—these would add some dimension to the performance. Encourage actors to use feline mannerisms, such as stretching, rubbing, cleaning face with "paws," to add life to the drama.

Note: The twins don't say much, but they play together on stage, sometimes annoying their brother and sister during the conversation. They can use their "paws" to play with a large stick, bat around a pinecone, ruffle each other's fur, etc.

Setting

The African plain

Props

★ A big stick for the twins to play with
★ Set details for an African plain, such as grasses, fake boulders, etc.
★ *Optional costume details*—lion tails, ears, whiskers

Cast of Characters

★ Papa, the hot-tempered father
★ Mimi, a soft-hearted but weak mother
★ Drew, the oldest child, independent and stubborn
★ Brandy, an adolescent with an attitude

Annoying younger twins
★ Fuzzy
★ Farrah

Helps and Hints for Middle Schoolers

Hanging out with the family is the norm for kids until adolescence. Preteens quickly gravitate toward friends as they grow older. This normal part of learning independence can cause a strain on even the sturdiest families. It's important to emphasize that while healthy friendships provide great training for adulthood, the family unit is still the primary way that God teaches children.

Some or even many of your students may come from dysfunctional or unusual combinations of families. Their experiences can skew their thinking about how God can use the people in their home to mold them into godly young adults. Affirm kids and the good things about their families. Don't accept the put-downs they verbalize about their parents or siblings. Gently, but firmly reiterate that no matter what the shape their families are in, God has a purpose in the family unit and will bring valuable lifelong learning from within the family circle.

Hold students accountable to live up to God's values and standards despite family failures. These young people will thank you once they can look back and see God's fingerprints on their earlier years.

Where's Your Pride?

When the scene opens, the family of lions is lounging around on various "rocks." They're scattered around the stage, distant from each other, each character using feline mannerisms.

Drew: *(bored)* Can I go out and pounce around with my friends? This is so boring.

Papa: *(reading a newspaper)* Are you kidding me? You're only 15! Who do you think you are?

Brandy: C'mon, Drew. You know the rules. *(sarcastically imitating)* "You can't go out past six o'clock on a school night." You know, you guys are the strictest lions in the pride. I *would* have to be born into *this* family *(rolls her eyes)*.

Mimi: *(stroking her daughter's fur)* Oh, sweetie . . . your father is just trying to keep you out of trouble. In a few years, you'll be on your own. For now, it's for your own good to live by our rules. *(pauses)* It could be worse. Look at the Carnivores down the street—they don't let their kids go out at all on weekends.

Drew: There you go comparing us again. Just because some parents are like heinous hyenas doesn't mean we've got it good. *(swats little brother who's trying to climb on him)* Get off me, you little cub-face! I'm not your climbing pole!

Papa: Now listen here, young man. You'd better treat your brother with some respect!

Drew: Yeah, like I'm supposed to learn from *your* example?

Papa: Oh, I see. I see how it is. Now you're the big man with the fancy comebacks. Who's paying for all those stalking lessons? Who's bringing home the chunks of meat? Last month we went out of our way to send you to Hunting School. And this is how you show your gratitude?

Mimi: Oh, stop, stop. We're a happy family, right? We're not supposed to fight like this. God gives us a family so we can learn from each other.

Brandy: But Mom, we're not the perfect family. So how are we supposed to learn anything from each other?

Papa: *(softening)* You know, your mom is right. *(pauses)* Drew, I . . . I blew it just now. Okay, listen. I'm not the perfect father. My dad always tried to be such a big shot . . . I've never been good at listening.

Mimi: No, honey, you're really a great father . . you're just tired a lot, and . . .

Papa: No! Don't go trying to cover for me again. That's the thing. You're a great mother to the kids, but you're too soft on everyone! You gotta stand up sometimes and show some spine, you know . . . raise your hackles. Roar a little now and then.

Brandy: He's right, Mom, you're a pussycat. Sometimes I wish you'd make a decision and stick with it. You let the twins do anything they want. And while we're on the topic of flaws, can you just once, Drew, listen to someone else's ideas?

Drew: *(interrupting)* Are you kidding me? I listen to you every single day go on and on about your little problems with all your little lioness friends . . . *(realizes what he's doing)*. Aw, man. I guess you're right. I don't listen.

Papa: Here's the deal, guys. I think we need to get with the truth that God uses even flawed families to teach us. I mean, what if our stubbornness can show us how much we need to submit to authority? I don't mean just you—I need to learn that too!

Mimi: Yeah, and you know how frustrated you get with the twins? Maybe God is giving you lessons in patience. Just think: When you have your own cubs someday, you'll be more prepared.

Brandy: I get it now! Just because we aren't the perfect family doesn't mean we can't learn from each other. Who would have thought God can use even stubborn lions.

Drew: I think the more stubborn the better. In that case, I've got the best teacher of all! *(swats at a twin half-playfully)*

Papa: Okay. So we've all figured something out. I've got a long way to go, believe me. It's going to take a lifetime for God to work on my pride, but I know it's what I need.

Brandy: Me too, Papa. And thanks for bringing home the great meat you hunt for us, Dad.

Drew: Yeah, thanks. *(pauses)* I guess you're not the lazy ol' guy I was telling my friends that you are.

Mimi: *(with uncharacteristic force)* Now listen here, young lion! You'd better shape up or I'll sharpen my claws on your behind! *(the others look at her with stunned surprise)* Hey, that felt pretty good! I'm getting it already!

Papa: I think we all have some improvement in the works. Drew, I've changed my mind. Go ahead and pounce around with your friends tonight.

Drew: No thanks, Dad. I've got some homework. But can I go tomorrow?

Papa: I was hoping you and I could catch a movie. I heard *The Man King* has a sequel now. It's probably not as good as the original but . . . *(They continue talking as they exit stage.)*

Curtain Call

Make the facts of the Scripture and the skit more personal and applicable by talking together.

★ **How can God use a family to teach you about life?** *(Parents' experiences can help you become wise. Their counsel and advice are useful. You learn how to get along with people and to grow despite difficulties.)*

★ **What can you do if your family isn't stable or a positive environment?** *(Learn what God says about trusting Him and do the best you can. Practice loving your family as best you can even if you don't receive what you'd like to from them. Use the gifts and good things God has given you—friends, church, Scripture, extended family—and let God mold you to be the person He created you to be. Learn what you don't want to do when you have your own family. Be the best example of Jesus you can to them.)*

★ **What can a family teach you about God?** *(that love counts for a lot, forgiveness is essential, even when others don't treat you right, God is good and doesn't change, God can change even the hardest situations through prayer and faith, even when people fail you and disappoint you, God will not, etc.)*

Time Waster and the Triangle Test

Bible Basis:

Acts 8:26–31, 34–35; 17:1–3;
1 Peter 5:12–14; 2 John 1

Memory Verse:

Do your best to present yourself to
God as one approved, a workman who
does not need to be ashamed and who
correctly handles the word of truth.
2 Timothy 2:15

Bible Background

The four passages in this lesson deal with different aspects of the burgeoning New Testament church. The first passage tells of an angel directing Philip to travel southward to Gaza. He met an Ethiopian official who had been reading Isaiah. This high-ranking government staffer had a clear desire to know more about the Scriptures. After he had been given spiritual insight into the truth of Christ's sacrifice, he acted on his new knowledge by being baptized. His time in the Word was clearly fruitful.

The second passage from Acts 17 describes Paul and Silas' travels through Macedonia and their visit in Thessalonica, where Paul spoke to the Jews in the synagogue. Paul took advantage of gatherings at synagogues to teach about Christ. Non-Jews would also attend and could be touched with the Gospel in this way. Paul skillfully used Old Testament writings to draw in his listeners before setting the Gospel before them.

Peter, disciple turned evangelist, concluded his letter encouraging the Christians scattered around Asia to stand unwavering in their faith in Jesus, no matter what persecution they would encounter. Such letters could make a difference for believers, particularly those young in their faith or cut off from a strong community of Christians. God's Word was their lifeline.

The overall theme of 2 John is holding tightly to God's Word. It's the critical element for growth and fruit in the Christian's life and essential to know and live by. John wrote this letter to affirm the truth of the Gospel—and the faithfulness of God's Word. John served as an elder, perhaps in the Ephesian church, in the later years of his life. His own life was a testimony of the value of keeping close to God's Word.

Summary

In the style of old-school radio melodramas, students use sound effects and voice acting to portray Time Waster, a character who can't seem to prioritize his time correctly. The purpose of this skit is not to promote legalistic lists of do's and don'ts, but to help students recognize the importance of prioritizing their time wisely.

Since this drama can easily be used with the script in hand, ask students who might otherwise decline to take parts. Other students can supply sound effects; these are essential to an effective and humorous performance. Allow time for students to practice vocal expressions of their lines and creating their assigned sounds before starting.

Tech-savvy students can download sound effects ahead of time if they choose; others can improvise using what's on hand in the classroom, and their own voices and bodies. Since the visual element is unnecessary for this activity, use a reader's theatre approach with everyone who's participating, sitting in a semicircle if possible.

Setting

An imaginary old-time radio sound studio

Props

★ A percussion triangle
★ Other items for making sound effects: alarm clock buzzer, water running, brushing teeth, humming a happy tune, books slamming shut, video game noises, basketball bouncing, feet walking, a cat screeching

Cast of Characters

★ Time Waster, a teenage boy or girl
★ Prioritizer, his "helper"
★ Radio Narrator
★ Teacher
★ Coach
★ Friends 1, 2, 3, 4

Helps and Hints for Middle Schoolers

Some preteens are equipped with a good sense of time and will keep to a decent schedule. Others are nearly clueless when it comes to organizing their activities and school requirements, much less knowing what time it is at a given moment. But these groups both need to internalize and practice the habit of building their lives around God and their relationship with Him. This takes intentional practice and good examples. And it will take awhile for many young teens. Each will have to find what works for him or her, from posting a note on her bathroom mirror to putting an alarm on his watch or cell phone as a reminder to read his Bible or have a quiet time with the Lord. Encourage your students to keep working at it, and offer them ideas of what works for you; let them share their ideas with each other, and mention useful devotional books, downloads, podcasts, etc., that can move them in the right direction.

Time Waster and the Triangle Test

Radio Narrator: *(in an over-the-top, melodramatic style)* To all of you out there in radio land, welcome to today's drama, *Time Waster and the Triangle Test.* Prepare to be amazed as we witness the rise and fall of our protagonist—a young man [woman] who cannot seem to prioritize his [her] calendar and put God first. The outcome will astound you! And now . . . we present to you *Time Waster and the Triangle Test!*

Time Waster: Arrgggh! I can't seem to fit this into my schedule no matter how hard I try. *(muttering)* I've got basketball after school, homework at the library until 5:30, a project due tomorrow, chores at home—*(interrupted by the sound of a triangle jangling).* Whoa! What's *that?*

Prioritizer: *(stage whisper)* Psssst! Hey there, T! It's me, Prioritizer!

Time Waster: *(confused)* Priori—who?

Prioritizer: Prioritizer. I'm the guy who helps you figure out what's most important. You know, the one who can save wasted time and make your life simpler. I heard you needed some help.

Time Waster: Since when do I need help with how I spend my time? I make good grades, I handle all my responsibilities, and my mom says I'm really organized. So, I guess *you're* the one wasting your time.

Prioritizer: Tell you what. If you pass a simple test, I'll leave you alone. Just prove to me that you can prioritize your time around what's most important, and I'm out of here.

Time Waster: *(annoyed)* I wish you'd go away right now. But all right, I'll do your test.

Prioritizer: Okay, here's how it works. You live your life for 24 hours, and I'll shadow you. Nobody'll know I'm even there. Whenever you make a time decision that isn't honoring to God, you'll hear this sound *(triangle rings).* At the end of 24 hours, if you've heard the triangle less than three times, you pass the test, and I'm history.

Time Waster: Sounds easy enough. Starting tomorrow, I'll prove I don't need your help!

Radio Narrator: Our hero T. has no clue that his troubles are just beginning. Let's listen to what happens as Prioritizer puts him to the test.

(Alarm clock rings.)

Time Waster: *(yawns)* Ah, what a great sleep. I gotta get going. *(Running water and teeth brushing, then humming a happy tune)* Bye, Mom! I'm leaving for school! *(Interrupted by the sound of the triangle)* What? Already? What could I have possibly done wrong already?

Prioritizer: Did you kiss your mom goodbye, or thank God for a new day, or eat something to give your body some energy? Do you think you're a machine or something?

Time Waster: Hey, you're pretty picky. All right, all right. You got me once. But it won't happen again. Hey, here's my class—I can't be tardy. *(Sound effect: footsteps)*

Teacher: *(dryly)* So today, class, make sure to complete both sets of questions before the test tomorrow. Any questions? See you tomorrow. *(books slamming shut)*

Friend #1: Man, she's giving us so much work. How about we split the questions, T.? I'll do half, you do the rest. We'll swap answers tomorrow morning.

Time Waster: Excellent idea. I'll take the first half. *(sound of triangle)* Oh, come *on*! Not you again. I thought you'd be impressed with how I was saving some time here!

Prioritizer: It's never a good idea to gain more time by doing something wrong. And cheating is definitely wrong. You've scored two infractions.

Time Waster: If I knew you were going to be a dictator, I never would have agreed to this deal. Okay, I've got another strike left. Just watch me—I've got it covered now.

(Sounds of video game playing)

Friend #2: T, you wanna play video games after school?

(basketball bouncing)

Coach: Wait a second, T. You have practice this afternoon.

Friend #3: What are you talking about? We agreed to go to the gym and lift!

Friend #4: *(sweetly)* Aww, T, you said we could study together at my house. My mom's getting a pizza . . . c'mon . . .

Time Waster: *(exasperated)* Wait! Everyone just stop trying to have a piece of me! *(mutters)* Looks like I totally over-scheduled. *(sighs in resignation)* I have no idea how to manage my time.

Prioritizer: Over-scheduled is right. And the most valuable thing you left out of your day? God! How can you have any kind of faith life if He's not even part of your daily routine? If God speaks to us through the Bible, you're pretty much shutting Him out.

Time Waster: Yeah, I see it now. I've been running around like this for months, and nobody ever showed me I've ignored my family, squeezed out my friends, and tried to please everyone except God. I give up.

Prioritizer: Don't worry, T. It's hard work to get your priorities straight. But you can do it. You just have to make time for it, starting with God.

Radio Narrator: So our young friend learned his lesson, with a little help from his friends. Thank you for joining us for today's program. Tune in next time when we discover just how dangerous it can be to rub a cat's fur backward. *(Sound of a cat screeching)*

Curtain Call

Bring this topic to the application level with some discussion and commitment to change.

★ **What time issues get in the way of making time for God?** *(school, family, sports, friends, too tired, etc.)*

★ **What is your biggest obstacle to making more time for God each day?** *(oversleep, don't remember, don't know what to do to have time with God, tasks take longer than I expect, no support at home or among friends, it's boring or not meaningful, etc.)*

★ **Name one change you can make this week to begin making more time for God.** *(Affirm all reasonable ideas. If students are open to the idea, consider letting them form accountability partners or small groups that will check up on each other, encourage, and support each other.)*

Mapping Out a Mission

Bible Basis:

Acts 16:6–15

Memory Verse:

"For my thoughts
are not your thoughts,
neither are your ways my ways,"
declares the LORD.
Isaiah 55:8.

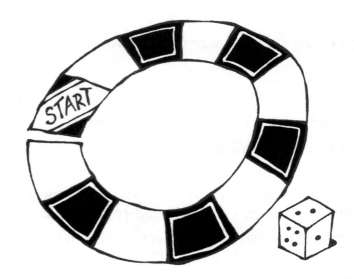

Bible Background

With our GPS devices and digital itineraries, our trips are foolproof, right? As Paul proceeded on his second missionary journey, accompanied by Luke, Silas, and Timothy, the events of his trip were not always planned in advance. In fact, the book of Acts records some important—and spontaneous—shifts in his itinerary.

Paul had determined at the onset of his travels to revisit cities where he had previously preached. In reality, it almost seemed like Paul was a pinball, being bounced in one direction, then pinging off in another, trying to find the right chute to head down. Being led by the Holy Spirit, Paul went where he believed God was directing him. It just took a few closed doors for him to finally discover the route and destination. This passage doesn't record Paul getting frustrated or tired of the seeming misguided direction he was taking. Actually, he seemed quite receptive to the redirection that he was given, and he kept his eyes and spirit in tune with God to figure out the right route.

Through the Holy Spirit's guidance, Paul ended up where God intended. He made contact with a small group of women and shared salvation with them. Lydia's proclamation of faith in Paul's message opened up ministry in a sector to which he otherwise wouldn't have had access. God clearly directed Paul's movements, although in an unusual and potentially perplexing manner. This narrative reveals to us how imperative it is to embrace the unexpected when we're following Jesus Christ.

Summary

Paul's second missionary journey took him to unexpected places. Using a paper floor map as a symbolic prop, two characters must survive an important journey. Despite obstacles and surprises, they bring others along with them on the road to Christ.

Setting

Imaginary Bible lands in a game board format (the spinner should be on the ground by the game board)

Props

- ★ A floor covered with game squares (see Note below)
- ★ Large spinner (made from poster board and markers or use a large one from a game like Twister)
- ★ Paper bag
- ★ Bible-time costumes for two male actors
- ★ Optional: CD player and road trip music

Note: This script requires a fairly large stage area. You can make squares with masking tape or, if you prefer, make squares out of poster board or large paper and anchor to the floor in a circular pattern. This would be a great project for one of your students who doesn't usually enjoy drama, but enjoys working with his/her hands.

Cast of Characters

- ★ Paul
- ★ Silas (try to find two boys with the ability to connect with the audience for the roles of Paul and Silas)
- ★ 3-4 extras

Helps and Hints for Middle Schoolers

Preteens are beginning that wild ride of adolescence when emotions and reactions can be so unpredictable. They might intellectually understand that God can lead them in unexpected directions, but experiencing it might elicit lots of emotional responses—complaints, anxiety, distress, objections to name a few. Try to communicate that the unknown is always a little scary, but once you've walked through a foggy time with God, you'll be less anxious the next time because you know He's dependable. And the end result of the journey might be better than anything you might have expected!

Mapping Out a Mission

*The set for this mini-play consists of squares on a symbolic game board (see Note, previous page). The two main characters, through dialogue, will merely suggest locations from **Paul's** missionary journey. **Paul** is sitting on a bench at the START square of the game board, tired and sweaty, while **Silas** is offstage ready to join him.*

Paul: Whew! Lystra doesn't exactly have the best truck stops. That restroom needed some serious cleaning. *(looks at the audience)* I'll bet you're wondering why I'm out here in the middle of this road. I'm Paul. My buddy Silas and I are on a major journey through Asia Minor. Why, you may ask? God called us to preach the good news of Jesus Christ to as many people as we can.

Silas: *(entering from the side, carrying a paper bag)* Okay. We're all set. I've got candy, a drink, and some beef jerky. Ready to go?

Paul: *(to audience)* That's Silas. He's my snack coordinator and best disciple.

*(**Paul** and **Silas** spin and move three squares to "Phrygia.")*

Paul: What a crazy name for a city. We're going to move everything in fast forward, so hang on . . . we'll be done in a second.

*(**Paul** and **Silas** move in silent, animated fast motion. They preach, hug, pray, and sing, and so forth to imaginary people for 10–20 seconds, and then freeze briefly to end the sequence.)*

Silas: Hey, those were great people. Lots of them decided to become followers of Jesus!

Paul: Yeah! That was an awesome stop. Let's see where we're going next. *(spins the spinner).* Cool! We're going to Galatia! *(Both hop two more spots to the "Galatia" square.)*

Silas: Are you ready, Paul? *(bows head)* God, empower us to encourage the Galatian church.

(Both repeat fast forward sequence, then freeze.)

Paul: Whoa. That church has some real issues to work out.

Silas: Maybe you should write them a letter?

Paul: Great idea! *(muttering)* Note to self: Letter to the Galatians.

(looks at the board and pauses) You know, instead of spinning the spinner this time, let's just turn west. Watch this. I'll spin and it will land on five. *(spins, it lands on the two).* Hey! Let me do it again. *(spins again—another two).* Rats! I'm sure God wants us to go west! *(spins a third time, and again spins a two).*

*(**Paul** shrugs; they hop two squares and read the instructions out loud: "Don't go to Mysia— go to Troas.")* Yikes! I guess God had this all figured out. I'll just follow directions this time.

(The characters proceed to spin three more times—first to Troas, then Macedonia, and then to Philippi. To make their journey more amusing, play road trip music in the background as they travel around the board. As they "travel," have 3–4 extras join them on each square, acting out friendly companionship, prayer, aid, or sharing meals.)

*(Music fades, extras leave the stage; **Paul** and **Silas** make their way back to their starting point.)*

Paul: *(arm around Silas)* Well, my friend, this has been an unforgettable trip. I'm glad that Dr. Luke was writing it all down. It was quite unusual. . . . You know, there's one place that we haven't visited yet.

Silas: Where's that?

Paul: The county jail. I would think prisoners there might need to know about God's love.

Silas: Um, I don't know, Paul. The jail? That sounds far out to me.

Paul: Maybe. We'll just let God direct our next expedition. I guess we can save the jail for another time. Wanna work on our singing instead?

Silas: Cool. But let's go get a drink first. I'm pretty thirsty. *(Both exit, singing.)*

Curtain Call

Bring the skit into the students' faith journeys through discussion and group interaction.

★ **When have you been on a trip that didn't take you where you expected?** *(Let students briefly share experiences.)*

★ **When your plans don't go the way you want them to, how do you react?** *(get mad, get frustrated, want to stop or go back, get stubborn and try harder to make things go your way, give up, have a tantrum, cry, etc.)*

★ **Why do you think God led Paul and Silas on such a strange trip, when they didn't get to go where they thought they should go?** *(God had a better plan. Maybe they didn't wait for God to tell them where He wanted them so they misunderstood. God knew that Paul wanted to do things God's way, so He knew they would eventually get to where God planned for them to be.)*

★ **Why would God lead us to unexpected places, like He did for Paul?** *(He can see the big picture of life that we can't see. He might want to do things in us or with us that we haven't thought of. We might be able to learn something or help someone that we wouldn't have been able to if we had gone the way we expected. God might test our faith or teach us to listen more closely to Him.)*

The Secret Life of Crimson la Rouge

Bible Basis:

Acts 21:10–14, 27-28, 31, 33; 23:11

Memory Verse:

However, if you suffer as a Christian,
do not be ashamed, but praise God
that you bear that name.
1 Peter 4:16.

Bible Background

Knocked down, chained up, arrested, and dragged around—just another day at the office for our buddy Paul. His intense abuse at the hands of Christ-haters is well documented in the New Testament. Some of Paul's own people, the Jews, turned against him in a fierce way once he declared his allegiance to Christ.

Besides physical abuse, Paul's opponents used verbal barrages to try to discredit and weaken him. Paul had to be on guard to respond to the accusations and error-strewn information his enemies used against him. But Paul didn't get defensive on his own account. He didn't attempt to salvage his reputation or guard himself unless instructed to do so by the Holy Spirit.

It's not surprising that Paul's companions were worried about his safety; they often forgot Paul's bond servant status to his Savior Jesus Christ, a connection that was far more binding than any earthly chains others might put on him. In Acts 21, Paul expressed his belief that he could die at any time. It is this level of commitment that marked his love for Jesus.

Paul, then, becomes an extraordinary model of sacrifice, made even more powerful in an age when following Christ—especially for young people—is full of misrepresentations and shallow promises of prosperity with no sacrifice required.

Summary

Crimson la Rouge always thought that being red would be easy. Isn't it supposed to be fun and exciting to be the color of scarlet in a crowd of boring beige? But Crimson shares her struggles openly, realizing that suffering just might be the best thing after all. This metaphorical monologue promotes an important discussion with middle schoolers about the costs of being a follower of Christ.

Setting

Empty stage

Costume

★ Plenty of red clothing for Crimson

Main Character

★ Crimson la Rouge—a recent convert to the world of red—is an allegorical symbol for a new Christian with much to learn about bearing the cross of Christ. Dressed in red, she should play the part with some campy melodrama.

Helps and Hints for Middle Schoolers

Being a Christian—and not hiding it—means standing out from the pack. For the majority of preteens, that's NOT where they want to be. Most young teens desperately want to blend in with the crowd. Having courage to be a public Christian often comes from finding others who are willing to stand out with you. Encourage students who go to the same schools or are in the same extracurricular activities to band together when it comes to being public about their faith. Explain that there are other subgroups: Goths, wannabe musicians, jocks. Christians are another subgroup that can have a cool identity and be true to their faith.

The Secret Life of Crimson la Rouge

*When the scene begins, **Crimson** is lying on the floor, despondent.*

(In melodramatic despair) I can't believe my sad, sorry little life! It all seemed so perfect at the time . . . I mean who wouldn't want to be the color red? Red! The finest color in the crayon box. The patriotic stripes on the flag. The shade of valentines and cherry drinks! In fact, someone stand up right now and tell me what you think of when you hear the word RED! *(**Crimson** stands up and listens to audience responses.)*

Oh, I had my choices, you know. I could've stayed brown, or changed to beige, gray, or safe pale blue. But no . . . I did it and went red. And now I know it's the hardest thing I've ever done. I keep thinking maybe I made a mistake.

I wasn't raised red, you know. I was born in Brownsville, Texas, to two really nice folks: Sienna and Russet. They raised me and my big brother Mahogany well. We were the All-American family. We even drove a Ford Khaki. Can anyone guess what street we lived on? *(fields answers from the audience . . . Tawny Street? Cinnamon Lane?)* Nope, it was Mahogany Avenue.

But as I got older, I realized I was missing something. I didn't want to be brown anymore. I met red folks who had a vision for the future. I could see they loved God more than anything. After a while of trying to be pink, I realized that I had to be all in or all out. So last year I decided to go red—100 percent, sold-out, fire engine red. I hung around with red friends, changed my name to Crimson la Rouge—even traded all my brown music for red.

You'd think that would be all good, right? I thought being red would make my life a lot easier. I expected everything would be more exciting. You know … never-ending happy feelings … an easy life.

But the red life isn't so rosy. First of all, I didn't realize that in some places, I stand out—I mean really stand out! I look around at my very beige school and feel like the only red one there. Being this color makes me different, and that's an uncomfortable feeling.

When I went red, my friends stopped hanging out with me, and *man,* that's been a sacrifice. It means telling the truth when I'd rather lie. It means staying home when I just want to join in. It means standing up when it would be easier to sit down. Why didn't someone tell me how *hard* being red could be?

Have any of you decided to be red? *(sits down again).* So I don't feel alone, can someone tell me why being red is hard for you? *(listens to audience).*

Well, I don't feel totally alone now. It helps when I think about that guy in Asia. Um, Paul. He went red. His experiences make my whining seem pretty silly. He was pushed around, yelled at, chained up in jail, beaten up, and kicked around. How come nobody tells you about that when you decide what color you want to be?

Yeah, well, I suppose I should quit feeling sorry for myself and get up off this floor. If I really think about it, I should be proud to wear the colors of my hero like Paul did. After all, he followed Jesus who wore red on the day He died, and because of that, I'll never be the same. *(exit)*

Curtain Call

Wrap up this monologue with the following discussion questions:

★ **How does it feel to stand out from the crowd?** *(uncomfortable, undesirable, not good, etc.)*

★ **Why is it hard to stand out from others when it comes to your faith in Jesus?** *(It makes you look different. People will pick on you. If you don't know how to answer their questions about what you believe, you feel stupid or like a fake. Once you're labeled, others won't accept you. If you mess up, everyone comes down on you for not doing things right or being perfect.)*

★ **How can your faith become cool, something positive to stand for?** *(when people other kids admire say they're Christians, when you cannot be pushed over by others' bad mouthing or mistreatment, when you do something cool like start a trend or organize an important event and others think it's worthwhile, etc.)*

★ **What kinds of responses can you think of when people put you down or make fun of you for being a Christian?** *(Point out famous people who were Christians like sports celebrities, actors, and actresses, etc. Ignore them. Show them lots of kindness and be friendly instead of reacting negatively. Students may have other worthwhile ideas also.)*

However, if you suffer as a Christian,
do not be ashamed,
but praise God
that you bear that name.
1 Peter 4:16

From Bug to Beauty

Bible Basis:

Acts 9:15, 19b–22; 22:5b–15

Memory Verse:

So then, just as you received Christ
Jesus as Lord, continue to live in him.
Colossians 2:6

Bible Background

Paul's story is a radical one. Originally named Saul, he was a devout Pharisee, trained in Jewish law, with a zealous ambition for wiping out heretics who believed in Jesus Christ. Being a devout Jew, he believed that Christians were dangerous to his beliefs and traditions, so he single-mindedly persecuted believers in many cities.

It was on a trip to Damascus to find and arrest more Christians that Paul had a personal encounter with the resurrected Christ, and it changed his life permanently. God chose Paul as his witness to both Jews and Gentiles, and his missionary adventures brought many to Jesus Christ. Up to that point, Christians had not been very active in spreading the Gospel outside the Jewish faith. But Paul was a dramatic example of going into all the world; he spoke about Christ to Jews, Romans, and Greeks, working diligently to convince his own people that God wanted the Gentiles to be saved on an equal basis with the Jews.

Paul used all his experiences and skills to evangelize. He traveled to many regions to teach and admonish, and he wrote letters to the established churches to further disciple them and correct errant behavior. As the writer of almost half of the New Testament, Paul's life is a radical testimony of how God can permanently change lives.

Summary

A butterfly is a metaphor for the radical changes that God makes in a believer through His transforming power. Monarch—a butterfly with an attitude—tells her audience she will never be the same again. From cocoon to color, she shows us how God changes us from the inside out.

Setting

Modern stage backdrop

Main Character

★ Monarch—a butterfly who has undergone an astonishing transformation through the power of God. (Depending on the skill and preference of the performer, Monarch can wear a traditional butterfly costume—wings and all, or convey the butterfly concept more abstractly through the script and body language.)

★ Monarch will need three audience members to help her tell her story.

Props

★ A brown/dark-colored sleeping bag

★ A blanket large enough to partially conceal a person

★ Butterfly costume, or alternately a colorful sheet or scarf draped across the shoulders and held in the hands to simulate butterfly wings.

★ Antenna headband (optional)

Helps and Hints for Middle Schoolers

The metaphor of a butterfly is appropriate in so many ways for adolescents. Their physical changes mirror the spiritual transformation God desires when we come to Him as new, Christ-changed believers. But expect that your preteens are going to have ups and downs in how they see themselves and their lives. Give them affirmation about the positive changes and maturity you're seeing in them, and plant plenty of hope and encouragement in them, assuring them that God is metamorphosing them into amazing beings, despite the discomfort and uncertainty they feel in the process.

From Bug to Beauty

*(**Monarch**, a newly-formed butterfly, begins her monologue by walking on stage mumbling to herself. The sleeping bag and blanket are already on stage.)*

Oh . . . oh . . . *(languidly stretching her back and adjusting her "wings", she looks at audience and realizes she's not alone).* I'm sorry! I'm still getting used to these fabulous wings. They're brand new, and I hardly know what to do with them! *(stretches and sighs again)*

I suppose an introduction is appropriate. My name is Monarch. It's my new name, for a new me. You wouldn't have recognized me just a few days ago.

Obviously I'm a butterfly. I have so much freedom now—I can hardly believe it. Yesterday, I flew back and forth from one side of the neighborhood to the other practically all afternoon just because it felt so good. But I wasn't always this way.

If . . . if you wouldn't mind, I'd like to tell you my story . . . but I need some help along the way. Would several of you help me out?

*(**Monarch** chooses three volunteers from the audience and brings them up on stage, introducing each by name. She instructs two to stand on the side and leads the third to center stage.)*

A long time ago, I was pretty lost. I existed in a dark, lonely place. My world was cold and lifeless. It probably was a little like this . . . *(She tells the first volunteer to climb into the sleeping bag and lie down.)*

I felt buried under the soil in a cocoon of sadness and emptiness. I didn't know who I was or if my life had any meaning or purpose. I had no idea what lay ahead of me.

But I'll tell you a little secret. When you're living in a dusty, moldy, brown sin-cocoon, you get a little comfy. I got used to it. I thought everyone in the world just had to live that way, and I might have stayed there if it hadn't been for the miracle just around the corner.

*(**Monarch** peeks down at the sleeping bag and stage whispers.)* How are you doing in there?

Not long ago, I was just hanging around in my dark and sinful world, not really happy, but not sure what else to do. All of a sudden I felt something new . . . a tugging at my heart. It was . . . like a stirring that I'd never felt before. I suddenly knew it was a fresh beginning! Right then I knew I was ready to shed my old life for something beautiful. Slowly, the brown world began to fade.

(She motions the other two helpers over and helps them hold up a blanket in front of the "cocoon." The first volunteer climbs out of the sleeping bag behind the blanket and throws it into the audience. All three helpers then leave the stage.)

Can you imagine my surprise? I had never known anything but a tunnel of darkness and being all alone. Then, suddenly, I was crawling into the sunlight, seeing hope for the first time. That's what kept me going on, out of the darkness. What an astonishing miracle! I knew this wasn't an ordinary transformation. I couldn't have done it myself. No, it was my Creator. The One who had designed me for life and joy had transformed me and brought me hope. I was ready to fly! *(She gives a small whoop of joy.)*

Believe me when I tell you it isn't all sweetness and light. Flying into the sunlight is sometimes scary, and there've been times I wondered if the old life was easier. But when I feel the beautiful wings I've been given, I have a huge sense of hope and freedom. I know I would never undo my metamorphosis. I want to give you one thing to think about. If you've ever wondered about your cocoon . . . just imagine the possibilities.

(She gracefully swoops offstage.)

Curtain Call

Help your students process the concepts through discussion and group interaction.

★ **What are some "cocoons" or comfort zones in your life?** *(friends, sanctuary of my bedroom, Internet friends and surfing, music, sports, etc.)*

★ **Why not stay in the comfort zone?** *(because that's not what God created us for, there's so much more to be and do once we have freedom in Christ, a comfort zone is really a place of death and decay instead of life and hope, etc.)*

★ **What kind of transformation do you think Monarch was describing?** *(spiritual, emotional, changes in physical being, growing up, etc.)*

★ **In what ways do you feel or have you felt a transformation happening to you?** *(changes in body, new thinking capacity, new skills or abilities, better understanding of life and myself, etc.)*

★ **What promises does God make to you and me about the persons He wants us to become?** *(be a new creation, leave behind the old and sinful ways, have a new start, have a purpose greater than ourselves, that after He forgives our sins He forgets them, that we can grow to become more like Jesus, we can be free of the old things we once did or were chained to, etc.)*

★ **What changes has Jesus made in you?** *(Listen eagerly to students' responses, but don't press them to share.)*

Who Needs a Pinky Toe?

Bible Basis:

1 Corinthians 12:14–27

Memory Verse:

Now you are the body of Christ, and
each one of you is a part of it.
1 Corinthians 12:27

Bible Background

The church at Corinth asked some of the same questions we do today: Who's the most important member of any given church? Am I just disposable? Would anyone notice if I disappeared? The apostle Paul realized that some of the more conspicuous gifts, like speaking in tongues, might be thought of as superior and as a result, some folks began to feel overlooked. Paul makes use of a metaphor, comparing the church to the human body where all parts are needed to function properly.

Paul's analogy of the body was one of his favorites. In 1 Corinthians, he does not suggest that our unity costs us our individuality. In fact, the concept of "equal parts" requires us to fulfill a very specific role. Like a living organism, the church seeks the kind of interconnection that leads to perfect balance.

Being human, it's not surprising that some church members would think they're more valuable or important to the functioning of the organization. And others whose gifts are meant for behind-the-scenes use, can be made to feel—or choose to feel—insignificant. Both these attitudes are wrong. God's concept of the church is that each person is endowed with the specific gift He chooses. To think more of yourself because of your gift is pride. To undervalue your contribution is to discredit God's wisdom in assigning gifts.

The beauty of the diversity of gifts God has handed out is that when used together as He purposed, they create a symphony of honor to Him and service to the body and beyond.

Summary

In this allegory, characters are human body parts who argue over their importance in planning a youth group retreat, only to discover that no one is unnecessary or "optional" in the body of Christ.

Encourage actors to play up their body part using exaggerated or noticeable body movements. Suggested actions are inserted in the beginning of the script as ideas. Actors need to use discretion to prevent distracting the other actors and the audience from the script, but can add more energy and humor with their interpretations of their body segments.

Props/Setting

★ A half-circle of chairs on the stage facing the audience

★ Costumes are optional. You can omit costumes altogether, letting the script speak for the characters. However, it might add a silly touch to design an allegorical costume or a hat holding a cardstock body part image. For example, Leggy could wear a headband supporting a drawing of a hairy leg, and so forth.

Cast of Characters

★ Eye-Man, a big shot with egocentric tendencies

★ Leggy, a strong-willed risk taker

★ Miss Heart, a patient, steady soul

★ Thumb-Thumb. a young, eager teen

★ Elbow, a sometimes annoying adolescent

★ Mr. Mouth, a natural servant-leader, reasonable and kind

★ Pinky Toe, suffers from an inferiority complex

Helps and Hints for Middle Schoolers

The teen hierarchy begins to separate into tiers during middle school as youth characterize themselves and peers based on physical characteristics and social skills. This can be disastrous for many, as they're labeled because of their height, social skills, athletic ability, etc. Your youth group should be a place where everyone has equal value, even if the back row is their refuge. You'll help them realize the importance of all the members of the body primarily by how you interact and include them in the group.

Continue to emphasize that God's endowment of gifts isn't usually about outward appearances or social skills. He gives gifts that are meant to work together, not as individual elements.

As adolescents move into this introspective and often painful stage of development, they can either gain an inflated view of their abilities and importance, or feel unneeded and unwanted. Your message that each member is essential and valuable will reap a great result. You'll be cultivating the next generation of church members and leaders in the process.

Who Needs a Pinky Toe?

The scene opens with seven members of a youth group milling around their meeting place.

Mr. Mouth: C'mon everybody! Gather round, gather round—we need everyone's help to plan the retreat. *(The group gathers, sits in a half-circle facing the audience)*

Eye-Man: *(eyeing the group)* I don't know why all of us need to plan this. Me and Leggy did the whole thing last year all by ourselves, and it was the bomb.

Elbow: *(elbows Eye-Man)* What are you talking about, Eye-Man? You mean it *bombed*! You guys just took over without getting any of our input.

Mr. Mouth: *(exaggerates mouthing his words)* Hold on, Elbow. Last year *was* a little stressful. Eye-Man and Leggy had some great ideas, but it did feel a little . . . imbalanced.

Thumb-Thumb: *(twiddles thumbs)* A *little*! All we did was watch movies and go hiking. That's perfect if you're an eye or a leg, but what about the rest of us? A whole bunch of us here can contribute great ideas to the group.

Miss Heart: *(places hand over her heart)* Mr. Mouth, what are your plans for the retreat? I think we all have a role to share in the planning.

Mr. Mouth: I'm glad you asked. Yes, this year we're going to make sure all our talents are recognized. Let's start with you, Pinky Toe. What would you like to be in charge of at the retreat?

Pinky Toe: *(has removed shoes and is wiggling pinky toes)* Oh, gosh. I don't know. I've never been in charge of anything before. I . . . I don't think I'd be any good. It's okay if Leggy or Eye-Man is in charge. I'll hang out in back.

Miss Heart: *(sympathetically)* Listen, Honey. You have lots of skills—you just don't know it! Don't be so hard on yourself! I know for a fact that we would've fallen flat on our faces last month if it hadn't been for you keeping us balanced when we stumbled over that rock.

Eye-Man: She's right, Pinky. We actually do need you, after all.

Pinky Toe: Really? Well, okay, I can try to help. Maybe we can try some toe wrestling?

Thumb-Thumb: What about me? What can I do?

Leggy: You? You're not nearly as important as some of us, but I guess you might be good for "thumb-thing." *(Laughs.)*

Mr. Mouth: Whoa, hold on. We all know you have a really important ability, but walking isn't everything, you know. Thumb-Thumb can get us everything we need—right within arm's reach. None of us can really get hold of things the way he can, right? *(Makes a hand sign with fingers and thumb while **Thumb-Thumb** smiles.)*

Leggy: What about Elbow? He was a pain last year; he just went around poking all the girls.

Elbow: Hey! I can't help it if I have a tendency to bump people. Give me a chance, will ya'? Seriously, Mr. Mouth. I'd like to contribute something this year.

Eye-Man: I'm not sure I like this. I'm used to being in charge, and now I'm feeling kinda . . . kinda disposable.

Mr. Mouth: No way! This isn't about any one person being the most important. It's obvious we all have important roles. We couldn't make it without every part.

Pinky Toe: We all just gotta do what we were made for.

Miss Heart: No kidding! If I were the only one in charge, we might be a little too soft.

Elbow: I guess if there were nothing but elbows here, we wouldn't be able to shoot hoops.

Thumb-Thumb: I get it now. But what happens if one of us isn't doing our part?

Mr. Mouth: Then it's up to us to encourage that person to get stronger. One strong part is great, but lots of strong parts are even better. So, whaddya say? Are we all in?

Eye-Man: You bet!

All: *(Like an athletic team, the group gathers in a circle. Each puts his or her hand in the center with the others.)* Go team! *(Hands are raised and all cheer.)*

Curtain Call

Give students a chance to interact with the lesson truth by discussing the skit and its meaning.

★ **Which body part—including those not portrayed in the skit—would you say you most identify with?** *(Allow students to answer if they wish, but don't force any to respond—answers can be humorous or serious.)*

★ **Do you know what is meant by "spiritual gifts"?** *(Listen closely to students' answers and correct any misconceptions. At their age, they may not have encountered this idea yet. Offer information and look up what the Bible says if they have no ideas. Emphasize that spiritual gifts are different from talents and skills, though they may go hand in hand.)*

★ **What kinds of gifts do you think God has given to people in our group?** *(Students don't need to mention names, but this can be an opportunity for affirmation and recognition of those who have quieter, less obvious gifts. Make sure you bring out all the gifts you've noted so no one is left out.)*

★ **What is God's purpose in giving each of us a specific spiritual gift?** *(to give us a way to contribute to the work of the church, to serve Him, to be part of a community that works together, to accomplish the purposes God has in the world, etc.)*

★ **What can you do if you don't know your gift or aren't sure you even like the spiritual gift it seems God has given to you?** *(If you don't know, pray and listen to God. Think about the things you like to do and feel drawn to. Ask for feedback from trusted people like friends, leaders, and teachers about what you're good at and where your strengths are. Observe others who serve in the church and see if what they do seems to resonate with you. If you don't like your gift, talk to God about it. Watch and wait to see how He could be planning to use you and your gift in new ways and places.)*

Sock It to Ya

Bible Basis:

Galatians 2:11–14; 2 Peter 3:15–16

Memory Verse:

Instead, speaking the truth in love,
we will in all things grow up into him
who is the Head, that is, Christ.
Ephesians 4:15

Bible Background

If you've ever wondered how to reconcile an old past with a new future, you can identify with the struggling church in Galatia. As former Jews, the Galatians were constantly trying to figure out what cultural laws to keep and what to throw out.

Paul found himself at odds with the Judaizers—an extreme group who argued that the old Jewish laws were required. Paul sought to teach the new believers that only faith in Jesus was necessary and that people of all backgrounds were welcome.

Paul and Peter, two leaders in the church, faced some conflict when they disagreed about church style. Yet Peter accepted Paul's reproof and the two remained on good terms, giving us a model of giving and receiving criticism with love, for the benefit of all.

This conflict demonstrates to us how confrontation should take place. Paul didn't complain about Peter's actions to others, or make a public declaration of the problem. He confronted Peter face-to-face. This is the best approach to working out differences in the church, and other places as well.

Paul's admonition was deserved, though Peter's behavior probably came out of a sincere desire to do what was right. We all have differences, and often the right choice is to accept one another's quirks and diversity. But when the issue is the essence of the Gospel, the situation must be dealt with honestly, constructively, and out of a desire for unity. When given and received correctly, constructive criticism keeps Christians in relationship with each other and with God.

Summary

A sock puppet wants to rescue her friend from a dangerous decision, but doesn't know how to tell him the truth. Advice from three friends reveals different ways to approach the dilemma. In the end, she realizes that speaking the truth in love is always the best decision.

Setting

A box-style puppet theater, or a homemade stage (an old sheet and PVC pipe, a piece of fabric strung between two walls, etc.)

Props

★ Five puppets—three male and two female—that can be adapted to fit the script.
★ Foam packing peanuts

Cast of Characters

★ Lindy, the main character
★ Connie, a friend
★ Sammy, a friend
★ Alex, a friend with a hammer
★ Mr. Olsen, a teacher

Helps and Hints for Middle Schoolers

With social skills that are still quite raw, middle school students may want to speak the truth in love but lack the finesse to do it. The best way to help them develop this ability is to practice. Use real life situations and brainstorm ways to tell someone the truth without hurting their feelings. Role-play in small groups; girls with girls and guys with guys. Prompt students to watch for examples of what works and what doesn't. Over time, as their awareness grows, their understanding and skill will develop. Remind preteens that this concept isn't about telling someone how to do things your way. It's about alerting someone to a harmful or potentially dangerous direction they're taking. Reinforce and model how prayer is always the first step in constructive criticism.

Sock It to Ya

Lindy: *(to herself)* Oh, my . . . *(heavy sigh)*. Oh, dear! What AM I going to do? *(shuffles back and forth across the stage)* Relax, just relax . . . calm down. It's okay, really. *(Looks out and notices an audience, surprised)* AAAHHHH! You scared me! You probably can see that I'm in an awful mess. My friend, Alex, is about to make a terrible mistake. He's building a new house, and he wants to use *foam!* Can you believe that? He's sure foam is the best material, but I know it will be a disaster. The building manual says to use tough materials. How can I tell him the truth without making him mad? *(hears noise offstage)* Shhhh! Someone's coming! Please don't say anything!

*(**Connie** and **Sam** puppets enter.)*

Connie: Hey, Lindy! Whatcha doing?

Lindy: Oh, hey, Connie, Sam. I thought you were Alex. Maybe you two can help me.

Sam: Sure, what's going on?

Lindy: My friend, Alex, is building a new house, and I think he's making a terrible mistake. He wants to build it out of foam! How can I tell him that would be a disaster without hurting his feelings?

Connie: His feelings? That's the stupidest thing I've ever heard. Girl, you should just blast him with the truth. Get it right out there. Tell him it's a stupid idea. Foam? Ha!

Lindy: But, Connie, he's my friend. I don't want to make him feel bad. Isn't there some other way to tell him without being so mean? What do you think, Sam?

Sam: I sure wouldn't tell him if I were you. I'd mind my own business. You don't want to mess up your friendship by saying anything to upset him. Let him build his house without interfering.

Lindy: But he could get hurt!

*(**Connie** and **Sam** shrug and exit, talking about **Lindy's** problem as they leave.)*

Lindy: *(to audience)* What do you guys think? Whose advice should I take? *(accepts audience input, then hears more noise offstage)*. Hey, here comes Mr. Olsen, my chemistry teacher. Maybe he can help me.

Mr. Olsen: *(whistling, enters)* Hello, Lindy. You're looking nice and . . . fluffy today. But you look a little depressed. What's up?

Lindy: My friend thinks that building a house with foam is the best choice, but I know from reading the building manual that it's not a good idea. One person told me to tell it to him straight and someone else said to just ignore his situation. What do you think?

Mr. Olsen: Have you thought about telling him the truth, but in a loving way? I mean, give him a truthful answer, but do it in a way that shows you care about him.

Lindy: I don't get it.

Mr. Olsen: Just think of it this way. Telling someone the truth is very important. Your friend needs to know that building his house out of foam could hurt him. But he also needs to know that you're on his side.

Lindy: Well . . . it would be easier to do it the way Connie or Sammy suggested.

Mr. Olsen: Maybe, but it's better to do the right thing than the easy thing. *(Hears hammering noise offstage)* Hey, here comes Alex. I know you can do it! *(exits)*

(From offstage toss bits of foam peanuts into the audience while making hammering noises. Alex, foam bits stuck to him, enters with a hammer.)

Alex: Whew! Construction is hard work!

Lindy: I wanted to talk to you about that, Alex. I know you're excited about your new house, but before you get too far, can I share something important with you?

Alex: Sure. What's up?

Lindy: Building a house out of foam blocks may seem like a good idea, but the building manual says that it might be dangerous. I wouldn't be a good friend if I didn't tell you the truth.

Alex: Really? You think I'm making a mistake?

Lindy: I care about you, Alex. Can I help you brainstorm a new plan? Maybe we could talk with a pro and figure out a way to make your house even stronger. I'll help you!

Alex: Whoa, Lindy. I'm really disappointed. *(pauses)* But I can see your point. Would you really help me?

Lindy: Of course! Here . . . give me that hammer. Let's figure out a better way together. *(The two characters exit while discussing their new plan.)*

Curtain Call

Make the skit and Scripture practical by discussing the ideas presented.

★ **What kept Lindy from talking with Alex about his foam house at first?** *(She didn't want to make Alex mad or hurt his feelings. She didn't know what to do.)*

★ **Being concerned for someone's feelings is a legitimate reason to hold your tongue. So how do you know when to speak up about someone's actions or decisions and when to keep your lips sealed?** *(Speak the truth in love when someone is doing something that could hurt themselves or others; speak the truth in love when someone is living in disobedience to God's Word. Only give constructive criticism in significant situations, not when it's about fashion sense or what a person likes to eat for breakfast. Know what the Bible says and follow its example. Pray and let God give you the go-ahead or tell you to stop.)*

★ **How should you take constructive criticism when someone else gives it to you?** *(Judge how much they care about you and their reason for telling you before you react. Consider how their words match up to the Bible and God's character so you can see whether they're right or not. Don't react right away but think about it first. Talk to them some more to find out why they made the criticism and where they got their advice.)*

★ **What's the main idea behind giving or taking constructive criticism?** *(to become more like Jesus, to learn to live God's way, that if we're honest about ourselves we can be more reasonable about our choices and how they might affect us and others, to be truthful and loving above all, etc.)*

Looking for Mr. J

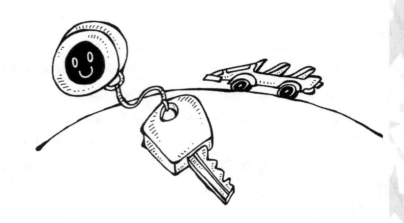

Bible Basis:

1 Thessalonians 4:14-17; Titus 2:11-14

Memory Verse:

Live self-controlled, upright and godly
lives in this present age,
while we wait for the blessed hope—
the glorious appearing of our
great God and Savior, Jesus Christ.
Titus 2:12b-13

Bible Background

With new churches sprouting up all over the place, the apostle Paul was one very busy guy. He had many new churches to watch over, straighten out, teach, and encourage. Like many of Paul's new churches, the Christians in Thessalonica and Corinth were growing in numbers—and they had plenty of questions. Timothy and Titus, two of Paul's assistants, were sent back to these young churches to strengthen and support the believers there.

Many had questions about Christ's return, and Paul responded with firm teaching. His emphasis was never on a detailed prediction of Jesus' second coming; instead he used Christ's return as a motivation for godly living. He also wanted believers to encourage each other when loved ones died about their hope for eternity.

The expectation of Jesus returning soon gives hope and perspective to our lives on earth as we go through hard times and dry periods and confront our sinful tendencies again and again. Knowing and trusting that the future holds an eternal glory with God Himself, we can maintain our persistent practice of faith. These passages help us see that living in the shadow of God's return spurs us on toward a God-honoring life. We can rely on the power of the Holy Spirit to keep our sights set on attaining godliness and pushing away the worldliness that is continually trying to wrap itself around our spirits.

Summary

This drama portrays a family anticipating the arrival of a special visitor. While preparations are made for his coming, the actors reveal the striking parallel between Christ's return and the anticipation of a fantastic event.

Setting

Interior of a modern home

Props

★ Home living room with several chairs or a couch, a bookcase or shelf, etc.
★ Miscellaneous housecleaning props, such as duster, broom, etc.
★ Set of car keys

Cast of Characters

★ Dad
★ Mom
★ Duke, 15-year-old son
★ Angela, 17-year-old daughter
★ Missy, 7-year-old daughter
★ Mr. J, special visitor, dressed in a suit and tie

Helps and Hints for Middle Schoolers

Preteens may have head knowledge that Christ said He will return, but their sense of time is more immediate. The future and the return of Christ seem very far on the horizon for this age group, so they may not take Christ's return seriously, just as one character in the drama doesn't. Help them connect this event with other things they've anticipated; compare it to waiting for something big, trying to be good in order to "deserve" a special Christmas gift, or consciously acting more mature so they can be granted a new privilege. In the same way, knowing that Jesus could come today or tomorrow should directly influence our choices, actions, and plans.

Looking for Mr. J

The scene opens as a family is excitedly cleaning their home. Each actor is involved in some preparation: straightening bookshelves, sweeping floors, cooking, and so forth. Only one family member, 15-year-old Duke, is lounging around, oblivious to the excitement.

Angela: *(while working)* I can hardly wait! I've had this date in my Palm Pilot for months—and now he's almost here!

Mom: Steady, Angela. Our visitor said he would be coming sometime between three and six o'clock—and it's only noon!

Dad: *(surveying his good work)* Well, I don't know about you, but this is the finest book arrangement I've ever seen. I even alphabetized the titles.

Mom: Hmm. Do you think that's a little over the top? Our visitor's supposed to have a surprise for us. Nobody said he would inspect our bookshelves.

Dad: Whatever. He's an important man. It's worth the extra work.

Duke: *(feet up, casually)* What's with all of you? We don't even know for sure if he's even coming. He didn't give a definite time. I think it's kind of rude to make us block out our whole day just to wait for him.

Angela: You'd better not be sitting like that when he rings the doorbell.

Duke: And what if I am? Will I get the evil eye or something?

Dad: Knock it off. You all finish this room. I'm going to rake leaves. *(exits)*

Mom: I realize you don't think this is important, Duke, but we need to be ready. Can you at least take out the newspapers?

Duke: Mom, this just isn't my thing. I can't pretend to be excited for something that might not even happen. I'm gonna go read my *Auto Trends* magazine. Coming up with money for my dream car is more important than housework. *(exits)*

*(**Mom** shakes her head, continues tidying for a few seconds, then lights dim and actors freeze for a short period to indicate a break in time sequence. When the scene reopens, everyone except for **Duke** is sitting with backs straight and proper on the couch or chairs. Everyone is silent. **Dad** checks his watch. **Mom** brushes off her pants. **Angela** and **Missy** are tapping their feet. They wait.)*

(A knock sounds at the door.)

Missy: Dad—quick! Get the door!

Mom: *(jiggles Dad's arm)* Go, go, honey! I'm too nervous!

*(**Dad**, composing himself, walks solemnly to the door, the others following him. With great dignity, he opens the door slowly. **Mr. J** is waiting, looking formal and stately.)*

Dad: Hello, sir. We're honored to have you in our home. Please, please, come in.

Mr. J: *(entering warmly, shaking **Dad's** hand)* I've been waiting such a long time to get here. I can't wait to share my good news with you!

Missy: *(stage whispers)* He's a lot nicer than I thought he'd be!

*(Everyone takes a seat and looks at **Mr. J**.)*

Mr. J: *(laughing)* Well, I'm glad you think so. *(pauses)* So . . . are you ready to hear my incredible news?

(All nod and agree.)

Mr. J: *(looking around)* Okay, but there's one little problem.

Dad: What's that?

Mr. J: I don't see him.

Dad: Who?

Mr. J: I don't see Duke.

Mom: Oh, Duke? Well, he couldn't be here today.

Mr. J: Didn't you tell him I was coming?

Dad: Uh, yes . . . of course, but he . . . well, he . . . *(looks down ashamed)* he didn't care.

Mr. J: *(sadly)* I see. *(pauses)* I'm so disappointed. I've been planning this moment for a very long time. But it's too late now. You see, I was going to give him these car keys to a brand new red Corvette. *(Everyone freezes as the lights go down.)*

Curtain Call

Move students from concept to personal application through discussion.

★ **Compare how Duke acted to how the rest of the family behaved.** *(Duke didn't care about the visitor. He didn't have any expectation of anything special. He was oblivious to the potential surprise, while the family was acting on their expectation and giving their all to prepare for the visitor. They had faith he would come and were acting like they believed it.)*

★ **Why was Duke disinterested in the expected event?** *(He didn't believe it was anything special. He had other things on his mind. He didn't want to put himself out preparing because he didn't know what he might get for it.)*

★ **How does this fictitious story compare to the expectation the Bible describes of Jesus' coming?** *(Even though we don't know exactly what it will be like or when it will happen, we need to be completely prepared and ready for the day He returns. Some people act like Duke, uncaring or not interested, because they don't believe Jesus will come or think it's too far off. Not being ready is a big mistake. We should expect Jesus to come anytime and live our lives like we're waiting for Him.)*

Givers and Takers

Bible Basis:

2 Timothy 4:9, 13;
Philippians 2:19–25; 4:18

Memory Verse:

Dear children, let us not love
with words or tongue
but with actions and in truth.
1 John 3:18

Bible Background

Think you have to be charismatic, wise, or saintly to offer encouragement? Encouragement is one of those gifts every one of us can give away. And that's not just a warm fuzzy idea. It's actually what God commands us to do throughout the Bible.

Philippians records a young man named Timothy doing minor, personal tasks for his friend Paul, such as fetching his coat or retrieving his books. Paul definitely needed some encouragement in this time period; he wrote the book of Philippians while jailed in Rome. Paul's main intent for this letter to the church in Philippi was to thank and encourage the church members. That didn't mean he couldn't benefit from a spot of encouragement himself!

The New Testament reveals that Timothy had a solid biblical upbringing by his mother and grandmother; his ordination is mentioned several times in the books of First and Second Timothy. But Timothy wasn't so focused on the missions that he didn't recognize the basic needs Paul had, and that that he, Timothy, could provide.

Despite some natural disadvantages, Timothy was a trusted companion of the apostle Paul. Timothy was young, and the Bible suggests he was naturally timid—not traits usually associated with ministers. Yet his life shows us that encouragement can come from the simplest places.

Providing encouragement is not a complex art. Timothy illustrated this well by hearing about Paul's situation and his needs, then acting to care for those needs. That's basically all encouragement is, but it blesses the recipient many times over. So whether you have the opportunity to provide for physical needs, pray for someone, or offer a listening ear, be available and attentive and you will be a blessing to those around you!

Summary

This activity uses no words at all—a challenging task for adolescents! Using pantomime and gestures *Givers and Takers* illustrates the difference between genuine acts of love and faked self-interest. You'll need to break kids into two groups: the "givers," representing acts of genuine love and encouragement, and the "takers," who live life to get all they can. Consider choosing the groups ahead of time (balancing personalities and styles) rather than letting kids select which group to join.

Setting

None

Props

★ Each group will determine props they could use to depict their chosen scenes. If you're in a home or large classroom with a range of household items to use, allow kids to choose appropriate props. If no items are available, encourage students to use pantomime in clever ways to convey their mini-scene.
★ Two signs: Givers, Takers
★ Spotlight

Procedure

Divide the stage into two sections with a sign hanging behind each: GIVERS and TAKERS. You can create a theatrical effect by using a spotlight to alternate between both groups from scene to scene. For example, while one side is performing a scene that demonstrates love and encouragement, the other side is frozen in the shadows, and so forth.

Provide each group with a list of situations and let them figure out how to pantomime the scene without words. Remind them that pantomime must be exaggerated rather than subtle in order to convey their point. They won't need to act out every single situation, but choose an equal number of scenes to alternate between. No scene should last longer than several minutes—especially when the other side is frozen!

Avoid micromanaging students' rehearsal. Allow them to independently test and practice different portrayals of the suggested scenes. Encourage them to use ideas beyond those listed in order to expand their critical thinking.

Helps and Hints for Middle Schoolers

Young teenagers long for encouragement. They bloom with it, and it's essential to their development. However, as much as they (like most of us) thrive on genuine encouragement, they can be clueless about how to give it. If preteens haven't had plentiful examples in their lives, they won't know how to show someone kindness. They may not even see who could use it since they tend to be self-absorbed. Give them a hand by being an example they can follow. Present opportunities to practice their own encouragement skills.

Givers and Takers

GIVERS:

- Tending to someone who is injured or sick

- Comforting a distraught friend

- Cheering and supporting an athletic performance

- Coming alongside during a hard task and patiently demonstrating how it's done

- Carrying something heavy for another person, or assisting during a strenuous task

- Laughing at someone's jokes—cheering up a group of friends with humor

- Assisting the frail or elderly

- Preparing and delivering a care package to someone (soldier, college student, homebound person)

TAKERS:

- Ignoring someone who is needy

- Laughing at a peer who is different in some way

- Sidestepping an obvious task, such as picking up trash or leaving a mess behind

- Refusing to assist the elderly

- Insisting on one's own method of doing something when others are trying to accomplish a task

- Monopolizing a conversation without letting others join in

- Gossiping about a friend

- Acting disrespectfully in a group situation and hurting someone's feelings

Curtain Call

Bring the topic of encouragement to a personal level and draw students into discussing personal application.

★ **How does it feel when someone does something kind for you?** *(great, good, like you matter, makes you feel valuable and special, etc.)*

★ **What kinds of acts of kindness can one person do to encourage another?** *(send a note, email, or text message, include them in a group activity, give a secret gift, help them out when they're having a hard time, pitching in to work with them, giving a hug or back slap to a struggling friend, sharing a talent without being asked, etc.)*

★ **Why do we sometimes choose not to encourage with an act of kindness?** *(fear of being misunderstood, not sure what to do, afraid others will make fun of you or make a big deal out of it, don't have time, don't care enough about others, don't see others' needs because we're too involved with ourselves, etc.)*

★ **What difference could an act of kindness make to a person who is hurting or alone?** *(give them hope, make them feel loved, give them a taste of Christ's love for them, change their outlook, encourage others to be kind also, etc.)*

Dear children, let us not love
with words or tongue
but with actions and in truth.
1 John 3:18

Topic Index

Theme	Page
Advice/Wise Counsel	18, 98
Authority	6, 38, 54
The Body of Christ	94
Cheating	78
Conflict	70, 98
Conversion	86, 90
Courage	30, 86
Creativity	22
Criticism	98
Discipline	42, 78
Encouragement	106
Evangelism	26
False Prophets	10, 50
Family	38, 74
Forgiveness	62, 70
Friendship	34, 98, 106
Gambling	58
God's Love	34, 46
God's Word	26
Holiness	10
Hope	70
Identity	46
Intimacy with God	46, 78
Mercy	70
Obedience	6, 38, 42
Parents	38, 74
Persecution	86
Prayer	34, 78
Priorities	78
Prophecy	50, 66
Purity	18
Satan	10
The Second Coming	102
Security	14
Sin	42, 70
Spiritual Gifts	94
Spiritual Transformation	90
Temptation	62
Time Management	78
Truth	10, 98
Wisdom	14, 18
Witchcraft, the Occult	10
Worship	22

Scripture Index

1 Samuel 8:4-10, 19-22 6

1 Samuel 28:1a, 3-19 10

1 Kings 3:5-14 14

1 Kings 12:3-16 18

2 Chronicles 5:12-13 22

2 Chronicles 17:1-10 26

Ezra 3:10-11 22

Esther 2:5-10 30

Esther 3:1, 5-6, 13 30

Esther 4:13-16 30

Psalm 34:17-18 34

Psalm 55:16-17 34

Proverbs 4:10-11 38

Proverbs 18:24 74

Proverbs 29:17 38

Isaiah 1:1-4, 11-20 42

Jeremiah 1:4-10 46

Jeremiah 14:14 50

Jeremiah 20:7-11 46

Jeremiah 22:3 50

Jeremiah 23:2, 26 50

Jeremiah 23:28-29 46

Jeremiah 28:15 50

Daniel 1:8-17 54

Daniel 5:1-18, 20, 21d-31 58

Hosea 14:1-7 62

Zechariah 6:12-13 66

Zechariah 9:9 66

Zechariah 11:12-13 66

Zechariah 12:10 66

Zechariah 14:3-4 66

Malachi 1:1, 5, 11 70

Malachi 2:8 70

Malachi 3:1-4 70

Matthew 6:6-8 34

Matthew 7:7-11 74

Luke 2:51-52 38

Acts 8:26-31, 34-35 78

Acts 9:15, 19-22 90

Acts 16:6-15 82

Acts 17:1-3 78

Acts 21:10-14, 27-28, 31, 33 86

Acts 22:5-15 90

Acts 23:11 86

1 Corinthians 12:14-27 94

1 Corinthians 14:15, 26-33 22

Galatians 2:11-14 98

Ephesians 6:1-3 38

Philippians 2:19-25 106

Philippians 4:6-7 34

Philippians 4:18 106

Colossians 3:20 38

1 Thessalonians 4:14-17 102

1 Thessalonians 5:17 34

2 Timothy 4:9, 13 106

Titus 2:11-14 102

Hebrews 12:5b-10 74

1 Peter 5:12-14 78

2 Peter 3:15-16 98

2 John 1 78

Action! Cool Theater
Correlation Chart

Title	Page	Scripture Reference	David C. Cook Lifelinks to God New Life College Press Reformation Press Wesley Anglican	Echoes The Cross
Patrick the Powerful and the Kid Kingdom	6	1 Samuel 8:4-10, 19-22	Unit 25, Lesson 1	Unit 25, Lesson 1
Light Fraud Speaks Out	10	1 Samuel 28:1a, 3-19	Unit 25, Lesson 3	Unit 25, Lesson 3
Wisdom Walks the Red Carpet	14	1 Kings 3:5-14	Unit 25, Lesson 5	Unit 25, Lesson 5
The Advice is Right	18	1 Kings 12:3-16	Unit 26, Lesson 7	Unit 26, Lesson 7
Jumping Jehoshaphat	26	2 Chronicles 17:1-10	Unit 26, Lesson 9	Unit 26, Lesson 9
Casino Babylon	58	Daniel 5:1-18, 20, 21d-31	Unit 27, Lesson 11	Unit 27, Lesson 11
Hope in the Hallway	70	Malachi 1:1, 5, 11; 2:8; 3:1-4	Unit 27, Lesson 13	Unit 27, Lesson 13
From Bug to Beauty	90	Acts 9:15, 19b-22; 22:5b-15	Unit 28, Lesson 2	Unit 28, Lesson 2
Looking for Mr. J	102	1 Thessalonians 4:14-17; Titus 2:11-14	Unit 28, Lesson 4	Unit 28, Lesson 4
Mapping Out a Mission	82	Acts 16:6-15	Unit 29, Lesson 6	Unit 29, Lesson 6
The Secret Life of Crimson la Rouge	86	Acts 21:10-14, 27-28, 31, 33; 23:11	Unit 29, Lesson 8	Unit 29, Lesson 8
Givers and Takers	106	2 Timothy 4:9, 13; Philippians 2:19-25; 4:18	Unit 30, Lesson 10	Unit 30, Lesson 10
Sock it to Ya	98	Galatians 2:11-14; 2 Peter 3:15-16	Unit 30, Lesson 12	Unit 30, Lesson 12
Dear Jeremiah	46	Jeremiah 1:4-10; 20:7-11; 23:28-29	Unit 31, Lesson 1	Unit 31, Lesson 1
I Don't Know, but I've Been Told	42	Isaiah 1:1-4, 11-20	Unit 31, Lesson 3	Unit 31, Lesson 3
Let's Put It on the Calendar	66	Zechariah 6:12-13; 9:9; 11:12-13; 12:10; 14:3-4	Unit 32, Lesson 5	Unit 32, Lesson 5
Fraud Buster, Private Eye	50	Jeremiah 14:14; 22:3; 23:2, 26; 28:15	Unit 32, Lesson 7	Unit 32, Lesson 7
A Tale of Five Piggies	62	Hosea 14:1-7	Unit 32, Lesson 9	Unit 32, Lesson 9
Danny Dawg & the Master G	54	Daniel 1:8-17	Unit 33, Lesson 11	Unit 33, Lesson 11
Courtly Courage	30	Esther 2:5-10; 3:1, 5-6, 13; 4:13-16	Unit 33, Lesson 13	Unit 33, Lesson 13
Time Waster and the Triangle Test	78	Acts 8:26-31, 34-35; 17:1-3; 1 Peter 5:12-14; 2 John 1	Unit 34, Lesson 2	Unit 34, Lesson 2
America's Next Best Friend	34	Psalm 34:17-18, 55:16-17; 1 Thessalonians 5:17; Matthew 6:6-8; Philippians 4:6-7	Unit 34, Lesson 4	Unit 34, Lesson 4
Where's Your Pride?	74	Matthew 7:7-11; Hebrews 12:5b-10; Proverbs 18:24	Unit 35, Lesson 6	Unit 35, Lesson 6
Don't Push My Buttons	38	Proverbs 4:10-11; 29:17; Luke 2:51-52; Colossians 3:20; Ephesians 6:1-3	Unit 35, Lesson 8	Unit 35, Lesson 8
Who Needs a Pinky Toe?	94	1 Corinthians 12:14-27	Unit 36, Lesson 10	Unit 36, Lesson 10
Worship Isn't for Spectators	22	2 Chronicles 5:12-13; Ezra 3:10-11; 1 Corinthians 14:15, 26-33	Unit 36, Lesson 12	Unit 36, Lesson 12